For the cover of this book, I photographed my seashore garden where I like to mix wild and cultivated flowers. Yellow coreopsis, orange butterfly weed, purple liatris, and silver beach wormwood scattered among the cosmos, zinnias, and other cultivated annuals and perennials make a cheerful summer display.

FRANCES TENENBAUM

GARDENING WITH WILDFLOWERS

- General rules of wildflower culture, including the importance of mulch and compost
- How to incorporate wildflowers into a traditional garden
- How to use them in "problem" places—along a driveway or in a back corner
- How to create a small meadow or woods on a suburban plot
- How to garden with native plants in a natural woodland, seashore, or wetland site
- Collecting plants from the wild to preserve them
- Conservation rules and protected plants
- How, where, and when to buy wildflowers—plus a list of suppliers

GARDENING
WITH
WILDFLOWERS

FRANCES TENENBAUM

BALLANTINE BOOKS•NEW YORK

In Memory of Frank

Library of Congress Catalog Card Number: 85-90869

ISBN: 0-345-32606-7

Originally published in hardcover by Charles Scribner's Sons

Book design by Amy Lamb
Cover photo by the author

Manufactured in the United States of America

First Ballantine Books Edition: March 1986

10 9 8 7 6 5 4 3 2 1

CONTENTS

INTRODUCTION

All the world loves wildflowers, yet relatively few gardeners grow them. When I first began this book, I had a three-part theory to account for this apparent discrepancy: the almost universal belief that wildflowers are hard to grow; the myth that you cannot grow wildflowers in anything but an exact duplicate of their natural environment, and the fact that there is very little practical literature on how to grow them.

Although today, months later, I still think that theory is valid, I am tempted to reduce it to one somewhat flippant statement: People don't grow wildflowers because they once planted pink lady slippers—and they died.

But all wildflowers aren't pink lady slippers, or other wild orchids, or rare and temperamental plants. Hundreds of beautiful wildflowers are actually very easy to grow. Often they do have to be planted in a duplicate of their native environment, but sometimes they don't. And where they do, the answer is to put the right flower in the right place, or to create the right place if you don't already have it.

This book is an outgrowth of my own experience as an amateur wildflower grower in two very dissimilar environments—the dry dunes and heaths of a sunny seashore and the shade of a traditional suburban property. More specifically, it was conceived out of my own inability to find satisfactory information in any single book about what, where, and how to grow wildflowers in a garden.

My problem was not the lack of books. But those by wildflower lovers were mostly personal reminiscences, and although delightful to read, were not practical enough for someone who really needed basic information. Those by experts frightened me away with their scientific terminology and constant warnings about the difficulties and complexities of growing wild flowers.

In spite of this discouragement, I did decide to make a wildflower garden, but now the more I read, the more my troubles were compounded. Often I had to refer to four or five different books to find instructions on how to grow half a dozen flowers. I was in even deeper trouble if a plant appeared in more than one book, since so many of the instructions were flatly contradictory—the black-eyed Susan is a pest no one should ever grow, said one author, while the next gave so many rules for transplanting it that one would think he was moving a rare wild orchid.

Many of the books I read were old and out of print, and therefore not easily available. Moreover, much of the nomenclature has changed over the years; this can be a problem both in research and in such practical matters as buying plants. For this reason, all of the flowers in this book are listed by both their common and botanical names; for the most part you can simply ignore the latter, but they are there for those times when you need them.

In the past, growing wildflowers was a hobby for expert gardeners, who chose to specialize in native plants, much as others specialized in growing roses, or dahlias, or other particular kinds of flowers. Today there are more and more people like you and me—whether we call ourselves gardeners or just people who like to garden—who, out of a rising concern for conservation and a human desire to relate to a simpler, more natural way of life, have become interested in wildflowers and wildflower gardening. This book, I hope, will fill the need for a practical introduction and guide to the subject.

SOME NOTES ON CONTENT AND ORGANIZATION
(OR WHY WASN'T MY FAVORITE FLOWER INCLUDED?)

Basically, this book deals with three aspects of wildflower gardening:

1. The wildflowers you can grow in your existing garden, either in beds, with or without other, cultivated flowers, or in areas where cultivated flowers do not succeed;

2. Wildflowers that you can use in existing natural environments, such as a seashore, a woods, or a wetland, without changing the environment to conform to the needs of formal lawns and plantings;

3. Wildflower environments that you can create, such as a meadow or a woodland garden.

Since growing wildflowers is very different from growing hybrid garden plants, a general introduction to wildflower culture will be found in Chapter One. However, the specific culture of different kinds of wildflowers also varies considerably, so it is important to look under the chapters devoted to special plants for a fuller description of how to plant and grow them. This is particularly important for seashore and woodland species.

Procuring wildflowers is also quite different from procuring cultivated garden flowers. You will find this information in the chapters on collecting and purchasing plants.

What exactly is a wildflower? Since it is neither easy, nor very productive, to find one perfect, all-inclusive definition of "Wildflower," let's just say that the flowers discussed individually in this book are, with a few noted exceptions, native American plants that have not been hybridized by man. Those plants that are not native— and this includes many of our most common roadside wildflowers— are immigrants that arrived here in one way or another from other shores, found their environment congenial, and simply took off on their own. The common oxeye daisy is perhaps the most familiar example of a well-assimilated immigrant.

Approximately one hundred flowers are described in this book. This leaves many hundreds more that, for one reason or another, have been omitted. I have purposely chosen to omit all orchids and most other rare and difficult flowers, although you could certainly argue with me here, for what is difficult for most people may be easy for you. Moreover, I *have* included a few flowers that are generally listed as "difficult," since in some of the very specific environments discussed in this book, they actually aren't hard to grow.

I have also omitted whole groups of native wildflowers because they are not adaptable for general use. Native alpines, for example, have a very limited range of growth in this country and cannot be grown successfully, except by experts, outside of this range (as opposed to oconee bells, or shortia, which grow wild only in a few isolated spots in the Carolina mountains, but which are easily grown in woodland gardens almost everywhere). Cactus plants are another native group that I have excluded as being too special. So, too, are the subtropical plants of Florida and the many California natives that depend not only on that state's unusual temperatures, but its rhythm of dry and wet climate.

I have also purposely omitted flowers that are too big or too weedy, or too small and insignificant to be widely useful in a garden situation; here again there will surely be great differences of opinion. Some flowers aren't included because I don't happen to like them and some because I don't know enough about them to describe their needs intelligently. For the most part, I have tried to include flowers that can be grown in most parts of the country, that are easily available from wildflower dealers, or that can be found and transplanted from the wild. This still leaves a great many flowers unaccounted for; to this, I can only say that this is primarily a gardening book, not a guide book or a wildflower encyclopedia. I apologize in advance if I have left out your favorite wildflower.

Whether you decide to grow any wildflower you happen to like (that will grow in the environment you can provide) or whether you choose to restrict yourself to true native American plants, or to only plants that grow wild in your area, is, of course, up to you. So is the decision as to whether you want to combine wild and cultivated species. Personally, I see no great virtue in depriving myself of shortia just because I don't live in North Carolina, or of *Rosa rugosa*, the magnificent beach rose, because it originally came from Japan. I think some wildflowers mix well with some cultivated flowers while others do not.

For me, the whole idea of wildflower gardening is that it is fun. I hope this book will introduce you to the fun of it too.

CHAPTER 1

Wildflower Culture

With roses to spray, hedges to clip, and lawns to weed and feed and seed, gardening sometimes seems to be more drudgery than delight. Yet somewhere out in the country and up in the mountains and down by the seashore, a world of beautiful plants manages to grow without the aid of noisy power mowers, chemical fertilizers, and gardeners who supply store-bought humus to replace the natural soil-building materials that they previously, laboriously, raked up and carted away.

To recapture for ourselves a part of the natural world of flowers is what this book is all about. In order to do so, we may first have to unlearn some of the garden practices we grew up on, and learn that in this case, at least, the easier way may be the better one.

Consider this gardening problem: The soil on the sunny side of your garage, where you want to make a flower bed, is thin, dry, infertile, full of rocks and gravel. In spring it is muddy, in summer baked and dry. Any experienced gardener knows that at the very minimum he must add lots of compost or peat moss and fertilizer,

---

ABOVE: Marsh Marigolds beside a pool. *(Arnold Arboretum)*

turn it all under to a depth of at least eighteen inches, mix it up thoroughly, and rake out the stones. The novice, not knowing any better, simply buys the plants he likes, digs holes in the dirt, and waits for his flowers. Very soon he learns what the experienced gardener knew all along: nothing will succeed in that bed but weeds.

The wildflower gardener has a different approach. Having decided that he doesn't want to go to the work of changing the soil, he looks for the flowers that in nature would grow in exactly that kind of environment—the brilliant orange butterfly weed, yellow wild indigo, purple coneflower, blue-eyed grass, black-eyed Susan, wild lupine, and that most beautiful of all native ground covers, bearberry, to name just a few.

Or take another typical gardening problem, which happens to have been my own: a rich, apparently fertile, loamy flower bed near a border of hemlocks and oaks. A little too shady, but not enough so to account for the poor showing, year after year, of even shade-tolerant plants. Fertilizer didn't help, and lime killed the Japanese iris, one of the few flowers that previously had managed to thrive. Our problem, to get right down to it, was the high acidity of the soil created by the near-by hemlocks and oaks. Fertilizer was useless because repeated applications of chemical fertilizer increases acidity in soil.

When finally we turned that bed from a perennial border into a wildflower garden and planted it with only acid-loving plants, *everything* grew and, furthermore, did so without constant attention from me. It was my first practical lesson in the virtue of working with nature, of selecting the right plant for the right environment. Since it was so successful, I began to look at the entire garden with a new eye.

The rose bed: every year an incredible amount of effort was spent in spraying roses, a smelly, disagreeable, and, we had learned, ecologically unsafe procedure. But even with all that spraying, certain of the roses were always badly mildewed, particularly my special favorite, Crimson Glory. Before now it had never dawned on me that a possible solution might be to remove the plants instead of coping with their pests. When I finally steeled myself to do so, leaving only the disease-resistant varieties, I found that in spite of a wet summer and no spraying, we had far less mildew than ever before, and with much less work.

But the worst trouble spot in our garden was right in front of the house where we wanted grass and foundation plants but where, no matter what varieties we tried or how much we improved the soil— in fact, no matter what we did—grass wouldn't grow and every shrub was sparse and sickly. Although eventually we came to believe my mother, who had said from the start that the two big linden trees in front of the house were the cause of all our troubles, we couldn't bring ourselves to cut down these shade trees. Of course, you know the end of the story: we finally did cut them down (discovering to our surprise that the house looked much better without them) and immediately every plant in the vicinity burst into growth as if released from prison, which is exactly what the trees had been to them.

For the wildflower gardener, the moral of the story is that you either grow plants that will flourish in the environment you can give them, or you change the environment. You don't waste endless effort in trying to make a plant grow where it doesn't want to be. Thus, if you want woodland wildflowers, but don't have the right conditions of shade, soil, and moisture, you first create the conditions and then buy the plants. In a way this may seem like the antithesis of gardening with nature, or of the no-maintenance gardening that growing wildflowers is supposed to be, but actually it isn't. To grow plants under adverse conditions means constant work, year after year. To make a new woodland or build a small pool or establish a meadow is certainly a lot of work, but once done and planted correctly, it really is *done*. Further maintenance is minimal.

First and last, the wildflower gardener works with nature. He doesn't fight it, although he may improve upon it since he is, after all, a gardener and not just a nature-lover. While the most dramatic way of improving on nature may be in creating a new environment, the more typical one that you unconsciously do all the time is to select for your garden only the best that nature has to offer—the butterfly weed and the wild indigo, but not the insignificant, uninteresting, or just plain ugly plants that usually grow in their vicinity. In other words, your garden will not be an exact reproduction of a natural wild area, but rather the distilled essence of its beauty.

By observing wildflowers in their natural habitat, we learn not only what flowers we can grow, and where, but something about how to grow them. For instance, the fact that most wildflowers grow from seeds and in competition with other plants should tell us two things:

That the flower that grows to perfection under these circumstances could, if given a nice little place of its own in a richer neighborhood, turn rank and weedy and produce more leaves than flowers; and

That in its natural habitat the roots of that flower probably had to wander far and wide as they developed (no potted or balled-and-baled root systems here, nor beds kept friable and free of tree roots).

Wildflowers, therefore, no matter how hardy they may eventually be, should be dug up and planted with even more care than cultivated flowers. Be sure to get as much soil and as much, if not all, of the roots as possible; don't let them remain out of the ground unprotected, and when you replant them, do everything possible to encourage the roots to recover quickly.

In other words, although the plant should *eventually* be treated neither better nor worse than in its natural state, it should be treated especially well when you transplant it. Even when planting in sand, I find it always helps to add compost or peat moss to the planting hole. In fact, the "worse" the plant's natural environmental demands, the more it needs babying in the beginning; it's obviously easier to put a new plant in a shady, rich, moist woodland garden than into a hot, baked, sandy spot.

Some other general rules of wildflower culture (you'll find more specific ones in the appropriate chapters) are:

1. No cultivating. Whatever weeding is necessary should be done by hand.
2. Always cover bare earth around the plants with mulch, at least until the existing vegetation takes over. Mulching will, among other things, reduce the need for weeding.
3. No chemical fertilizers. At the most, if you feel the need, you might use a very weak solution of liquid fertilizer. However, if you use compost and mulch with natural materials, you really shouldn't need to fertilize at all.
4. No weedkillers. But see the chapter on poisonous plants for an exception to this rule.

One of the most important things we can learn from observing the way wildflowers grow where man doesn't interfere with them is how to imitate the never-ending process of returning to the soil the materials that came out of it. Of course I am referring to making compost—the natural way to enrich soil, the one that has no polluting side effects as chemical fertilizers have been found to have, and the one that is certainly easier and cheaper than cleaning up everything and then going out to buy its packaged equivalent.

A few years ago I might have been brash enough to tell you how to make a compost pile. All I do is throw all the garden refuse into a pile, let it decompose, then use it. If the pile gets too big before it is ready to be used, I make a second. While I add to one, I use the other.

However, according to recent writings on the subject, this is all wrong. Many other methods are suggested, most of them involving huge expenditures of time and labor. Since I don't really understand half of what they are saying, I don't feel qualified to select one method and say, this is how to do it. Any current book or magazine on organic gardening will tell you more than you need to know about making compost.

One other thought: I am invariably asked how I keep a compost pile from becoming offensive and attracting animals. I have *never* had either of these problems, probably because I never throw anything but garden refuse on the compost. I assume "green garbage"—vegetable tops, coffee grounds, and other nonanimal matter—would be equally inoffensive.

For readers who want guidelines, rather than exact formulae, the following excerpt should be useful. It is taken from an article, "The Art and Science of Composting," by Anthony S. Taormina, a fish and wildlife biologist. It was published in *The Conservationist*, official magazine of the New York State Department of Environmental Conservation, through whose courtesy the excerpt is reprinted.

Compost refers to a mixture of various decaying organic substances such as leaves, garbage and manures which at some time are made available to fertilize the land. Mixtures of decaying organic residues may be confined into pits, boxes, trenches, holes or various other enclosures for esthetic, space or sanitary reasons. Or they may simply be scattered naturally about the land surface as are twigs and leaves in a woodlot or manure in a pasture. But whatever the materials to be composted, the compostables, the basic objective is to allow them to decay as quickly and orderly as possible so that their locked nutrients may be harmlessly and profitably released to the topsoil to nourish plants which in turn will nourish or otherwise benefit animals—man especially.

Some of the more important factors which influence the rate of decomposition are the following:

Size of particles: Smaller the better, shredding a real benefit.

Temperature: Warmer the better; ideal temperature in a compost pile about 150 degrees F.

Moisture: Compostables should be damp but not soggy.

Availability of oxygen: . . . Any action such as mixing or loosening which allows air to be in contact with the compostables will speed up the decaying process and also reduce unpleasant odors.

Avoidance of toxins: Toxic materials such as pesticides and other biocides as well as paints, certainly industrial wastes and unknown liquids should be kept out of your composting arena since they may kill or impair some of the delicate hard-working decomposers.

How you set up your composting arena depends upon a number of factors including where you live, your acreage, nature and abundance of the compostables and ecological acumen of your neighbors. Fortunately, composting may be accomplished successfully in a number of ways with infinite variations. From the following described basic methods you should be able to choose a technique that suits your particular life style.

1. Natural: The random scattering of plant and animal residues (leaves, branches, feathers, feces, urine, etc.) over fields and woodlots is the natural way decomposition and recycling occur. It is a very good system for those who have adequate acreage.

2. Sheet Method: The process of spreading a thin layer of manure over a field is known as the sheet method of composting, although farmers have been known to call it something else. I have found that thin layers of aquatic plants such as "washed up" eel grass or salt marsh cordgrass (as well as grass clippings, leaves, etc.) when spread between garden rows or under fruit trees, berry vines or rose bushes make an ideal mulch-compost. There are many variations to the theme depending on what is available to you.

3. Open Pit Method: One of the simplest backyard methods is to dig a series of shallow holes or trenches (2 to 3 feet wide; 1 to 2 feet deep) in your garden area into which your daily accumulation of compostables (mostly garbage and pet manure) are dumped. Certain birds and mammals such as starlings, jays, grackles, opossum, coons, cats and dogs may become regular visitors, depending on where you live. With the exception of dogs, which can either be fenced out or controlled by their owners, such animal use is generally unobjectionable. If rats are already common in your neighborhood they too may feed on certain compostables. However in the more than 20 years I have used this method, I have never seen a rat. In the summer it is desirable to regularly cover the compostables with thin layers of soil and lime not only to control flies and odors, but also to enhance the compost. You may plant seeds over the holes as soon as they are filled. Before the ground freezes in the fall be sure to dig enough holes to last through the winter. . . .

4. Covered Pit Method: Mobile—where open holes may be considered objectionable, take the bottom out of an old garbage can and place it over or in the hole you wish to fill (just deep enough so it won't blow

over). By keeping the lid on, birds, mammals and flies will be excluded. When the hole becomes filled, top it off with soil and lime and dig another one.

5. Covered Pit Method: Permanent—dig two pits each approximately 2 feet deep, 3 feet wide and 3 feet long, framing them with either stones, concrete blocks or planks, etc., 8-12″ above the ground. Cover with a lid and fill one first before starting the second one, remembering to mix and dampen. By the time the second one is filled the first pit should be well composted and ready for the garden, shrubbery, etc. Earthworms will become especially active in methods 3, 4 and 5, provided they are present. If not present, they can be introduced several months after starting the compost.

6. Top of the Ground Bin: Place a framework of either snow fence, chicken wire, wire fencing, concrete blocks, pole cribbing or similar "porous" material in a convenient location and gradually fill with compostables. A double bin can be made as suggested in method 5.

CHAPTER 2

Introducing Wildflowers to Your Garden

Modern gardening suffers from many of the same kinds of side effects of bigness and technology that have proved a mixed blessing in so many other areas of society. Labor-saving devices, such as power mowers, spreaders, sprayers, choppers, and clippers, do indeed make those jobs easier, although not necessarily pleasanter. They also tend to be noisy, malodorous, polluting, and expensive. And in the end they may not prove to be labor savers after all, since they lure us into doing jobs that are not always necessary, or necessarily desireable. The power lawn vacuum cleaner that sucks up leaves and long grass clippings also removes every bit of loose organic matter from the surface of the dirt, where it would have acted as a natural mulch and eventually decomposed into humus. Power cutters make it too easy to mold hedges into stiff unnatural shapes, when they might better have been allowed to grow into their own more graceful forms.

ABOVE: Three Sisyrinchiums, lovely members of the iris family. *(George Schenk)*

Similarly, as mass production makes well-grown, well-potted, quality-controlled plants available to millions of gardeners, virtually every roadside nursery is a supermarket carrying identical plants. Now that sod comes rolled up in strips and instant lawns replace the headache of trying to establish one's own weed-free turf, wall-to-wall grass is no longer a joke.

These are very real advantages and not to be sneered at. Unfortunately, they do carry a price tag in the form of standardization and monotony. And when spring planting is merely a matter of setting out six-packs of ready-grown annuals, or punching holes in plastic containers preplanted with seeds, or even laying out strips of seed-impregnated "mixed flower borders," gardening might better be called exterior decorating.

I certainly don't intend to imply that only the "serious" gardener deserves to enjoy the pleasures of flowers, or that the only way to achieve diversity and individuality in a garden is by planting wildflowers. On the other hand, since they are the subject of this book, wildflowers *are* one very good way of bringing individuality and a new sense of adventure and excitement into gardening, while at the same time encouraging the preservation and propagation of native plants. More and more varieties of bigger, brighter, sturdier zinnias are fine, but not all of us want only zinnias.

Equally important, perhaps more for many readers, is the fact that native plants, once established, are far less demanding than most hybrids. Since they are usually perennials or self-sowing biennials, they are also a lot less expensive and far less trouble than the annuals we are accustomed to purchasing each year to use as fillers after the first flush of spring bloom has passed.

EASY FLOWERS FOR SHADE

If you have never grown wildflowers before, this is a good place to begin. These shade-loving flowers will grow in average garden soil under exactly the same conditions that cultivated shade flowers require: in other words, light or moderate shade with some sun and reasonable moisture. Like cultivated plants, they won't do well in dense shade, but they will take quite a bit of sun if the soil isn't hot and dry. Taken as a group, they are even easier than the flowers-for-sun, since they won't become weedy if given a richer environment than they are accustomed to in the wild.

They are also especially desirable because there really aren't very many cultivated plants that will flower in shade, as witness the amazing development and popularity of the hybrid impatiens in the past few years.

Although I have purposely selected plants suitable for flower beds, keep in mind other places you might use these same specimens: interplanted with ground covers, in a shady rock garden, in a woodland garden, or even in a wet, *sunny* spot, if you can provide enough extra moisture. Flowers that are described in other chapters which would also be suitable for shady flower beds are indicated by an asterisk *. And don't overlook the possibilities of the nonspreading ferns*.

Because this is such a desirable, reliable group of wildflowers, all of them are easily available from wildflower dealers everywhere, as well as from many general nurseries.

CRESTED IRIS
Iris cristata

A low-growing, mat-forming plant, rarely more than six inches tall, but with large, light lavender-blue flowers. It blooms in early spring, but the leaves remain all summer, making it a neat, attractive plant for the front border of a shady bed. Because of its spreading nature,

Iris cristata

it is also useful as a ground cover or a plant for a shady rock garden. *Iris cristata* is easily grown and may be divided at any time, or increased by removing a small piece from the mother plant. The rhizomes should be planted close to the surface and NOT mulched heavily.

JACOB'S LADDER
Polemonium reptans

The flowers are a brighter purple-blue than the Iris, and the plant is a little taller, usually about a foot high. It also blooms in the spring. The foliage is pretty, but not dense enough to be considered a ground cover (and, in my garden at least, disappears sometime during the middle of the summer). It will thrive in sun, too, if given added moisture and mulched, and it makes a very pretty rock garden plant in the shade. A related cultivated species, quite similar, and the one usually offered by general nurseries, is *P. caeruleum*, sometimes called by the name Greek Valerian.

WILD BLUE PHLOX
Phlox divaricata

An absolutely beautiful light blue flower to grow in drifts among tulips and other spring bulbs. The foliage hugs the ground and the flower heads are held about a foot high on wiry stems, with several stems arising from each clump, making it showier, for that reason, than the two previous plants. Although it is generally an undemanding plant, it doesn't like very acid soil, so if you want to use it in a woodland garden instead of a flower bed, please read about acidity in the chapter on woodland gardens. Clumps are easily divided in the spring.

WILD GERANIUM (Crane's-bill)
Geranium maculatum

A very pretty pinkish-lavender flower with delicate, deeply notched leaves. The wild geranium (no relative of the *Pelargonium* that we know as the geranium) grows from twelve to twenty inches tall along shady roadsides in late spring. It is a very easy plant to grow in a variety of shady locations, and if it has any fault, it is that it tends to self-sow rather freely. But no more so than many cultivated plants, and it is easy enough to weed out the seedlings. The flowers wilt quickly if picked.

VIRGINIA BLUEBELLS
Mertensia viginica

Showy, bell-shaped flowers on strong, arching stems, from one to two feet high in spring. The flowers are pink in the bud stage and blue when fully open. *Mertensia* develops into large clumps, which may be divided. However, be warned: the tubers, which you start by planting under about four inches of soil, work down as the plant grows, and you will have to dig deep to avoid injuring the roots.

Mertensia has only one fault: its leaves must be allowed to ripen, a yellowing process that seems to take forever. Unfortunately—I speak from experience—if you get disgusted and cut them down, you can lose your entire planting. The solution is to place your plants carefully, behind a fern or another later-blooming flower of good size that will come into its full growth as the *Mertensia* dies back. Or tuck the foliage down where it can't be seen; just don't break it off.

WILD COLUMBINE
Aquilegia

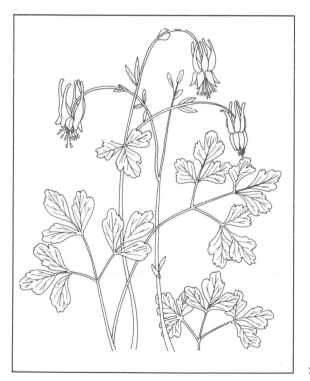

Aquilegia canadensis

The flower of *Dicentra eximia*, the wild fringed bleeding heart. *(Arnold Arboretum)*

There are many species of this well-loved native plant, the most commonly sold being the American Columbine, *A. canadensis*, which has red and yellow flowers with long red spurs. It grows from two to three feet tall in graceful clumps and self-sows generously. You can easily increase your collection by waiting for the tiny seedlings to appear and then moving those, rather than digging up the mature plants. It blooms in late spring in most areas.

WILD FRINGED BLEEDING HEART
Dicentra eximia*

SPIDERWORT
Tradescantia virginiana

Some people might dispute my inclusion of spiderwort in a cultivated flower border, because it does tend to have rather weedy foliage and can grow into very big clumps. However, that occurs mostly when planted in a wet, sunny place. In a shady garden, the bright blue flowers seem to me to be asset enough to compensate for any liabilities. Like the flowers of day lilies (although much smaller), the flower of the spiderwort lasts only one day, but there are so many buds on a single stem that the blooming period is extensive. One way to control the size of the plant is to cut back some (not all) of the foliage after the plant has finished blooming.

BEE BALM (Oswego Tea)
Monarda didyma

A tall, rather coarse red flower held well above its leaves. Use this at the back of the border where it will provide you with bright color and long bloom in the summer when very little else in a shady garden will be in color.

Note: When buying or collecting this plant, don't confuse it with its close relative Wild Bergamot, *M. fistulosa*, which is also known by the name Oswego Tea. Bergamot is lavender and grows in dry, sunny soil.

One might have the same objection to bee balm as to spiderwort, that it is a large spreading plant. However, it spreads fast in a wet sunny location, and the back of a shady flower border usually is quite dry. Besides, it is easily divided, and the spreading growth of many cultivated flowers doesn't stop a gardener from using them.

Monarda didyma

EASY FLOWERS FOR SUN

The biggest difference between easy flowers for shade and easy ones for sun is that some that thrive in sun could actually be *too* easy if you aren't careful where you use them. In their wild state, they usually grow under somewhat adverse conditions, unfertilized, in competition with other vegetation, and in rather poor, dry land. If you treat them too well by bringing them into a heavily fertilized, well-watered, sunny flower border, they may repay your kindness by turning rank and weedy and then crowd out your specimen plants.

If you have perfect growing conditions in a sunny border, you'll do better to save that bed for your cultivated plants and look elsewhere on your property for places to use wildflowers. (Or look under the chapter on plants for soggy, wet places to find flowers that will adapt to the rich, although drier, soil of a sunny border.)

The great virtue of the flowers in this chapter is that they *will* do well in less than ideal conditions, where cultivated plants will suffer. They also provide color in the garden and cut flowers for the house in summer and fall without the necessity of watering and fertilizing and all the other work that goes into growing cultivated flowers.

Although I can't tell you exactly where to plant these flowers in your garden, here are some suggestions:

1. The extreme rear of a flower bed where the sprinkler doesn't reach.

2. The typically long, narrow strip between a driveway and the side property line. If this area is contained, say, by a black-top driveway on one side and a fence or a hedge on the other, you can even forget the warning about planting in good rich soil, especially if you use only wildflowers, since they won't be able to jump their bounds or crowd out delicate plants. Usually this is a poor site for choice flowers anyway, because of too much traffic, the heat of the sun on a hard-topped driveway, and fumes from the cars.

3. On a rocky or gravelly slope, or a border of your property along the road, where it would be difficult to dig a good flower bed and a nuisance to mow the lawn.

If you are a new homeowner faced with the overwhelming job of landscaping everything at once, from foundation plantings to lawns to flower beds, you can put off some of the work by planting wildflowers along the back of your land without bothering to prepare a bed. This will allow you a few years to concentrate your efforts around the immediate area of the house and still give you a source of cut flowers. (See also the chapter on making a meadow.)

And of course, if your garden generally has poor, dry soil, you can plant these flowers any place, so long as they get sun.

Lastly, please remember that you should give all wildflowers a good start, no matter under what conditions of adversity they naturally grow. Dig a good hole, add peat moss or compost, and water them in well. Don't fertilize. In the sun weeds are always a problem. Either weed by hand until the wildflowers take over or use a heavy mulch. Don't worry about the frail little weeds; just go for the big gross ones that might crowd out your flowers. And don't cultivate; that just prepares the soil for a new invasion of weed seeds.

Most of these flowers are available from dealers or can be easily collected and transplanted.

BLUE-EYED GRASS
Sisyrinchium

Put this tiny, charming member of the iris family in a sunny spot where you can appreciate it, and where its narrow, sharp foliage won't be mistakenly mowed for grass. Its deep violet-blue flowers with bright yellow centers open one after another over a long blooming season in spring and summer.

Since it takes a sharp eye to spot a single blue-eyed grass, plant a few together; they will quickly spread into a good-sized clump. As long as it has sun, blue-eyed grass seems to tolerate almost any condition. It is very easy to transplant from the wild, even in bloom, which is fortunate, since you would scarcely find it otherwise.

Use it for a rock garden, along a path, or for naturalizing in any sunny place. Even good soil can't make it a weed. In the wild, one species or another grows virtually everywhere in North America. If you buy it, the variety usually listed is *Sisyrinchium angustifolium*.

BUTTERFLY WEED
Asclepias tuberosa

The butterfly weed is such a stunning plant that some garden catalogues list it as butterfly flower. By either name, the butterflies love it and it is a choice plant for any sunny garden. The flowers are bright orange in large, flat clusters, on twelve-to-twenty-four-inch stems.

The dark green foliage stays neat and attractive throughout even the driest summer.

Although the butterfly weed is easy to grow even in terrible soil, don't attempt to transplant a mature plant; it is virtually impossible to dig up the enormous brittle tuber without damaging it. Small plants can be dug up successfully, and both seeds and tubers are available from dealers. If you gather your own seeds, wait until the pods are just turning brown and remove the silken parachutes from the seeds before you sow them. Like most perennials, they will not bloom the first year.

WILD LUPINE
Lupinus

This is one of the most beautiful of all wildflowers for a sunny garden. The flowers are usually blue or white, sometimes pink. *L. perennis* is a native of the East Coast, growing in dry, nonfertile, sandy soil along the coastal areas and as far west as Minnesota and Louisiana. Texas Bluebonnets, *L. texensis*, the state flower of Texas, also grow in dry sandy soil. *L. polyphyllus*, a native of the Northwest, may reach five feet in moist soil, but will also grow, albeit not so tall, in a drier environment.

For some reason, I have never been able to find this extremely choice native plant listed in any seed or plant catalog; maybe I have somehow simply missed it. Although, like the butterfly weed, mature plants are not movable, you can transplant the seedlings. Be sure to take some soil with them. You can also collect seed. Get it when it is just barely ripe and plant it right away; again, take some of the soil from its native habitat.

CAROLINA THERMOPSIS
Thermopsis caroliniana

This is a plant you can safely grow in a good sunny flower bed. Use it toward the rear, since it may reach a height of five feet in rich soil. The spikes of large yellow flowers are very showy and are sometimes mistaken for a yellow lupine; not very surprising, since both are members of the pea family. Unlike the lupine, however, the Carolina thermopsis is sold by most wild flower dealers.

A shorter, bushier plant of the same genus, that grows in dry soil, is the Bush Pea, *T. mollis*.

PURPLE CONEFLOWER
Echinacea purpurea

Although the purple coneflower will grow very well in poor, dry, gravelly soil, you can safely use this in a good bed too, since it isn't at all weedy. The flower petals are reddish purple and droop downwards from a darker purple center cone. It is similar in appearance, although certainly not in color, to the black-eyed Susan, but far less common. Seeds and plants are carried by wildflower dealers.

BLACK-EYED SUSAN
Rudbeckia

There are several species of *Rudbeckia* that go by the name black-eyed Susan, but it doesn't really matter since it is hard to believe that there is any section of the United States where you could grow this western prairie flower and not find plenty to collect for yourself. They are very easy to transplant, and although biennial rather than perennial, they self-sow readily. The flower is desirable enough to have been hybridized into the gloriosa daisy.

Coreopsis lanceolata

LANCE COREOPSIS
Coreopsis lanceolata

You may already have this one in your garden, since it is an accepted "cultivated" plant as well as a wild one. Because it doesn't grow rank and weedy, you can use it in a good sunny border as well as in its native dry, sandy or rocky soil. It has bright yellow flowers with wide rays and makes a most attractive display throughout the summer. There are several species of coreopsis, but this one and the similar *C. grandiflora*, a self-sowing biennial, are the best for dry, sunny areas. Lance coreopsis is a perennial; it is easy to transplant from the wild, and may be divided in the spring. The prettiest of all coreopsis, *C. verticillata*, has an entirely different appearance. It is a small, bushy plant with fine-cut leaves, and from June to September is covered with small starry yellow flowers. (See color photo) It has recently begun to appear in good nurseries.

NEW ENGLAND ASTER
Aster novae-angliae

Of all the many species of aster, this is the one most often offered for sale and most widely cultivated in home gardens. It is a tall plant and should be used toward the back of a flower bed. However, since it grows naturally in rather wet soil, given drier conditions it may not tower quite so much, which is fine with most gardeners. The flower heads are larger than those of most wild asters and range in color from purple through purple-pink to white. It is easily transplanted and available from all dealers.

If you are collecting from the wild, you'll find many other asters which you may like. One of my favorites is the Heath Aster, *A. ericoides*, which grows in extremely poor dry soil, rather tall, with lots of small white flowers. It isn't that it looks very special in the garden, but the flowers make a wonderful substitute in bouquets for baby's breath, a cultivated plant that has never succeeded for me.

CHAPTER 3

Ground Covers

In the ideal wild garden, there is no place for bare dirt. The woodland earth is covered with leaves, pine needles, twigs, rotting wood in all stages of decomposition, and other forest litter; bogs are covered with sphagnum peat and other mosses; grasses grow in the meadows; even at the seashore, the dunes behind the coastal beach are stabilized by deep-rooted grasses and salt-hardy plants.

Earth that has no form of organic covering material is rock or dust or mud or beach or desert.

In our own gardens, taking our cue from nature, we use grass to cover most of our bare dirt. (No one who has ever moved into a new housing development can forget the muddy mess of the first spring before the lawns became established.) In many ways, grass is the ideal ground cover but we don't want it everywhere; and in some places where we do want it, it won't grow. So year after year finds us reseeding thinning patches of lawn and, throughout the growing season, weeding and cultivating the flower beds, creating a neat and attractive home for more weed seeds to sprout.

ABOVE: A groundcover planting of naturalized violets and primroses. *(George Taloumis)*

Or we give up the whole expensive and laborious process and turn to ground covers. Probably our initial reason for planting ground covers is to escape the drudgery part of gardening, but it also turns out to be better garden culture. With all that careful cultivating and raking, we not only disturbed shallow plant roots, we defeated the long-term process of returning to the earth the organic material that came out of it. Lately the gardener's urge to tidy up his yard has come under scrutiny as a possible cause for the proliferation of the devastatingly destructive gypsy moth. A U.S. Forest Service study in cooperation with agencies in the states of New York, New Jersey, and Connecticut, is aimed at determining whether the spread of the caterpillars is inadvertently encouraged by homeowners whose cleanup of all dead branches, brush, and other "litter" deprives natural predators—particularly blue jays, grackles, calosoma beetles, and white-footed mice—of their protective cover.

By shading the soil, ground covers reduce the need for watering. By smothering weed seeds, they reduce and eventually eliminate the need for weeding. By providing shelter for fallen leaves, twigs, pods, and other organic matter, they enrich the soil naturally. And by their ability to grow in places where grass or flowers don't survive, they reduce the expense and effort of gardening against the grain of nature.

It is almost impossible to imagine any landscape design that couldn't be improved upon by the use of groundcover plants. Some of the suggestions that follow will be obvious to you, but it is my hope that they will inspire you to look over your own property with a fresh and critical eye. Is all that wall-to-wall grass the most interesting way to treat your land, and is it worth the time and effort? Most of us are so used to coping, or struggling, with our landscape plan as it already exists that we hardly think of how it might be done differently.

Ground covers underplanted among shrubs and tall perenials conserve moisture, shade roots, smother weeds, and mask the dying foliage of bulbs and flowers. Near a house they absorb the spattering of rain that can erode the soil and mar painted walls or trim.

Where grass won't grow or is hard to mow, ground covers are the natural alternative. Use them in the shade of a shallow-rooted tree, on steep or uneven banks, to cover unsightly or dangerous tree roots, or in any area where nothing seems to flourish but weeds.

Almost everyone has at least one of those narrow or oddly shaped areas, really too small to turn into a lawn, yet ticky-tacky if made into a flower bed—the triangle between the driveway and the front path; the corner of the lawn that is used as a shortcut; grassy areas around and between individual plantings of trees or shrubs. Only you know where your problem spots are, but when looking over your landscape design think of the possibilities, from the viewpoint of esthetics and maintenance, of connecting up isolated units into a single unit of design.

Choose ground-cover plants to suit your site. No matter how much you love the tiny woodland partridgeberry, it makes no sense to buy it for a mixed underplanting of violets and ferns, both of which will hide it from view. Size, height, rate of growth, as well as the more obvious requirements of sun or shade, must figure in your selection of groundcover plants.

If your groundcover area borders a lawn or a flower bed, be sure to select plants that are not rampant growers or seeders. Some of the prettiest little creeping plants turn into impossible weeds if they move into a nearby lawn. Try them instead in an area that is bounded by a driveway or a path. Watch out, too, for the noncreeping invaders; no simple barrier like a driveway will suppress the reproductive urge of the common blue violet, which explodes its seeds as much as fifteen feet in every direction. On the other hand, its wealth of flowers and lush green leaves, as well as its propensity for reseeding itself, are just what make the common violet a good ground cover in a large natural landscape where lawns and flower beds do not exist.

Since it is nature's way to cover bare earth with growing plants, it should hardly be surprising to find that there is a wealth of wild ground covers for every situation. More surprising is our willingness to restrict ourselves to only the ubiquitous pachysandra and ivy and the one or two other plants generally sold as ground covers.

"Ground cover" is a subjective term; I have seen ground-cover lists that included shrubs up to six feet tall and flowers that lose their foliage in late summer. Without belaboring the point, or even trying to find a consistent set of criteria, my own definition of a ground cover is a plant that may or may not have a significant flower, but *must* have attractive foliage which, if it is deciduous, lasts all summer, at the very least; the plant must grow in a creeping or spreading manner or multiply by reseeding itself freely.

The plants I have selected are generally hardy throughout the United States, assuming you can meet their cultural requirements as indicated. Some, however, are northern plants that may not do well in California or the South. But gardeners in those areas have many other native plants that will not survive northern winters.

In the lists that follow, plants with an asterisk * are described in detail in other chapters.

This is by no means a complete list of possible ground covers, but a selection of unusually choice ones. Except for bearberry and the vines, all of these ground covers need shade to some degree. A number of them are described as requiring acid soil. Be sure to read about acid soil in the chapter on woodland gardens.

Evergreens	*Deciduous Plants*
Bearberry	Barren Strawberry
Ferns*	Bunchberry
Galax	Crested Iris*
Oconee Bells*	False Lily-of-the-valley
Partridgeberry	Ferns*
Trailing Arbutus*	Foamflower
Wild Ginger	May Apple
Wintergreen	Violets*
	Wild Strawberry*

VINES (including some to avoid!)

Used as ground covers, vines are suitable only for large areas. If you have a small garden and want to use a wild vine, it can be trained to grow up a wall or clamber over fences. In that case, however, be sure to note the habits of the vine very carefully before making your selection.

Bittersweet	Virginia Creeper
Everlasting Pea	Wild Clematis
Honeysuckle	Wild Grape*
Nightshade*	

EVERGREEN GROUND COVERS

BEARBERRY
Arctostaphylos uva-ursi

Height: three inches. Bearberry is a woody, prostrate sub-shrub with small, shiny, dark green leaves that turn bronze in winter. The tiny pink flowers are followed by bright red berries that look like cranberries but are mealy and inedible. Although it may be somewhat slow getting started, it spreads quite quickly once it is established, and makes a magnificent dense carpet in baking sun or light shade, in sandy, gravelly, infertile, moderately acid soil. Use it on banks or slopes or areas bordering a road or driveway.

Bearberry is one of the finest of all native ground covers and grows wild in many sections of the country. In the Rockies it is called kinnikinick. A California relative is manzanita. Although presumably it was named for the bears who eat its berries, obviously deer like them too, since another name for bearberry is deer food.

Bearberry is often found growing in pure sand, along cindery railroad beds, covering rocky exposed slopes, and in similarly inhospitable places. However, don't let this ruggedness fool you—bearberry is one of the most difficult plants to move and should *never* be dug up during any part of the growing season. (Actually, it is one of the valuable native plants that shouldn't be collected at all, except under certain unusual circumstances. See the chapter on collecting and conserving wildflowers.) The only successful way to transplant bearberry is by cutting frozen sods in the winter and laying them, covered by a mulch, in a previously prepared bed. You would be much better off to take cuttings in early summer and root them in a mixture of peat moss and sand.

I have never seen bearberry listed in wildflower catalogs, although I have occasionally found it in a nursery. The best way to acquire it is to buy potted plants. As you can imagine, they are somewhat expensive, but once you have them established, you can increase your supply by making your own cuttings. If you have the site for it, bearberry is well worth the trouble or expense.

GALAX
Galax aphylla

Height: six inches. The white flower spike of the galax, up to twelve inches tall, blooms in June, but its leaves are what the plant is all about. They are relatively large, round, and leathery, a rich dark green that turns russet in fall and winter, held aloft on stiff stems. Don't be put off by the fact that the leaves of the galax are gathered by the millions for funeral wreaths.

Although it is a native of the southeastern mountains, galax is perfectly hardy throughout the United States provided it has acid soil. It needs shade and indeed will tolerate fairly dark shade. While it is another slow-starter, it is easy to grow and if left alone will spread readily. Use it in foundation plantings along with acid-loving shrubs like rhododendrons, azaleas, and laurel, or in a woodland garden. Its leaves make a very handsome contrast in front of ferns. All dealers carry it.

PARTRIDGEBERRY
Mitchella repens

Height: one inch. The fragrant white flowers are followed by bright red berries. The shiny oval leaves have a distinctive white strip down the middle. Partridgeberry is an easy, fast-spreading ground cover, but it will never become a pest. It grows in shade or half-shade in rich, woodsy soil.

The only possible problem is that you will miss seeing it altogether if you grow it with larger or coarser-leaved plants. Use it in a woodland garden, or at the edge of one, or in a shady rock garden. And be sure to take some in for the winter for a terrarium or the popular Christmas partridgeberry bowl.

All dealers carry partridgeberry, but if you collect it yourself, be sure not to pull up the individual vines, but to cut good-sized sods. You can easily increase your stock by taking cuttings in midsummer and rooting them in sand and acid peat moss. Remove the seeds from the pulp in the fall and try planting them in a sand-and-peat mix.

WILD GINGER
Asarum

Height: four to twelve inches, depending on the species. A handsome plant with large heart-shaped leaves. The strange brown flower at the very base of the plant is an interesting oddity, but otherwise of no

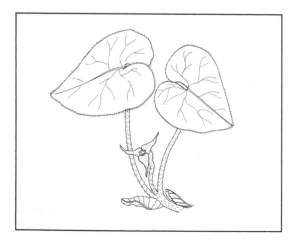

Asarum canadense

consequence (since you can't even see it unless you get right down on the ground and lift the leaves to look). Wild ginger will grow in even dark shade, but it must have moisture. Use it at the foreground of your foundation planting, in a woodland garden, a shady rock garden, or almost any other place where you can appreciate its beautiful leaves.

Although it isn't related to the true ginger plant, the root of the wild ginger tastes something like it and can even be candied. Most nurseries offer both *A. canadense*, which has light or gray-green leaves, and *A. virginicum* (sometimes listed as *A. shuttleworthi*) which is more truly evergreen and has dark shiny, sometimes mottled, green leaves.

Wild ginger makes an excellent dense ground cover in a surprisingly short time but is still easy to keep under control in restricted areas.

WINTERGREEN (Checkerberry)
Gaultheria procumbens

Height: two to six inches. Although bigger in all respects than the partridgeberry, wintergreen is not as dense a ground cover as the other plants in this group—a factor to consider when you are using it. It is extremely pretty, though, with dark glossy green leaves and white flowers followed by red berries. It wants shade and acid soil and will even thrive in quite dry soil, although it will be rather sparse. Use it in a woodland garden or a shady rock garden, but don't hide it in a foundation planting.

If you have soil that is acid, wintergreen is a very easy plant. All dealers carry it, and if you have a friend with a woods, it is also easy to transplant. It, too, is best taken in sods, and you can increase your supply by division. Be very sure to keep the new plantings well-watered until they are established—a precaution, by the way, that holds true for just about anything you transplant.

DECIDUOUS GROUND COVERS

BARREN STRAWBERRY
Waldsteinia fragarioides

Height: three to eight inches. Barren strawberry has small yellow flowers and blunt, three-part leaflets. It grows in dry, or moist, rich acid soil, in light to medium shade.

The most obvious distinction between this and the true wild strawberry is the lack here of any berry. Other differences are the color of

the flower, yellow instead of white, and the fact that the barren strawberry has no runners. This last is a real advantage if you want to
restrict the plants to a small area. Barren strawberry is tall enough to
be used with a variety of wild and cultivated ground covers and is
useful in almost any place so long as you have moderately acid soil.
It is carried by some dealers and is easily transplanted from the wild.

BUNCHBERRY
Cornus canadensis

Height: four inches. Bunchberry is one of the most beautiful of all
ground covers, but don't bother trying it unless you can meet its
rather fussy demands—cool, very acid, rich soil and shade. Its natural
range is from Alaska to Greenland, and as far south as West Virginia
and California (but in the cool woodlands and mountains at the southern part of its range).

The bunchberry, with its white flowers followed by red berries,
looks just like a miniature dogwood; in fact, the two are members of
the same family. If you have the right place for it, it is a strong-
growing plant and will spread quite quickly. If a friend will spare you
some, transplant it in sods. However, you are better off, and so is the
plant, if you buy it. All dealers have it.

Cornus canadensis

FALSE LILY-OF-THE-VALLEY (Canada May-flower)
Maianthemum canadense

Height: four inches. This is a very fast-growing, neat plant that makes a thick, pretty colony in almost any shady place, including average garden soil, although it is at its best in rich, woodsy, somewhat acid soil. It is particularly good in a foundation planting, provided it isn't smothered by taller-growing species, and combines well with rhododendrons and azaleas. It is easily purchased or transplanted in sods.

FOAMFLOWER
Tiarella cordifolia

Height: eight inches. If you don't insist that a ground cover be evergreen, this is probably the best and most useful of them all. (Actually, it is classed as a semi-evergreen, depending upon where you live.) It has clouds of feathery white flowers in spring, large handsome leaves all summer, and is easy to grow. With enough moisture, it will spread quickly, and it is very easily propagated by transplanting the runners that appear in summer. It prefers light shade. Use it anywhere you like, but it is particularly good with small bulbs or in sweeping plantings beneath deciduous trees.

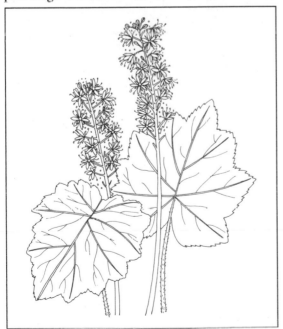

Foam flower

May apple makes a luxurious ground cover in a large area. *(George Taloumis)*

MAY APPLE (Mandrake)
Podophyllum peltatum

Height: twelve to eighteen inches. A large plant with unique, umbrella-like leaves hiding a solitary flower, which is followed by a yellow fruit. The May apple grows in light shade under deciduous trees. It does not do well in very wet, acid soil.

May apple is an excellent ground cover because the leaves are held horizontally, and because it makes fast growth. However, note the height; this is not a plant for very small areas or where you have other plants you want to show off. It's excellent, however, for hiding the yellowing foliage of daffodils and other large bulbs, or the dying-back foliage of plants like Virginia bluebells.

VINES

BITTERSWEET
Celastrus scandens

If it were not for its marvelous red-orange berries, which brighten fall roadsides and will last in your house most of the winter, bittersweet could be a vine to avoid like the plague. Even so, be forewarned: bittersweet is a strangler and not even tall trees are safe from its ropy hold. It is not suitable for a small property and should be kept away from any valuable shrubs or trees. Plant it in a wild area or near a fence where you can keep an eye on it, and don't hesitate to prune it back if it appears about to get out of control. The berries last on the vine well into the winter and are a very good source of food for birds.

EVERLASTING PEA
Lathyrus latifolius

It's probably stretching a definition to call this a ground-covering vine, and frankly I've never seen it growing that way—in the wild, it always grows in a tangle, climbing over underbrush and shrubs—but its flowers are so beautiful and the plant so easily grown that it's worth making an exception to any rule to include it.

The everlasting pea is a European immigrant and garden perennial that has escaped cultivation and now grows wild over much of the eastern half of the United States. The roots of the plant stay in one place, which ought to make it easy to transplant; however, I've never been able to get near them, since all the plants I've seen are entwined in the thorniest of wild blackberries. The very large flowers, like pink, blue, or white sweet peas, are held on stiff stems and last a long time when cut for the house. Unlike sweet peas, though, they have no scent.

The easiest way to obtain the everlasting pea is to collect its seed pods. Plant the seeds where you want them to grow; they sprout almost immediately. Any soil will do, but the more sun, the more flowers.

HONEYSUCKLE
Lonicera

Most varieties of the sweet-smelling honeysuckle are desirable vines for the wild garden. The exception is the Japanese honeysuckle, sometimes called Hall's honeysuckle. It is evergreen, fast-growing, and truly ground-hugging, all qualities that seem desirable. However, it will absolutely take over and crowd out everything in its path, and it is almost impossible to eradicate once it has taken hold. I would strongly urge you not to use it. It is sold by virtually all nurseries, sometimes for quite a price, considering what a pest it is.

VIRGINIA CREEPER
Parthenocissus quinquefolia

For some reason I don't quite understand, many people confuse Virginia creeper with poison ivy; perhaps it is because they grow in the same neighborhoods and because both turn such a gorgeous flaming red in the fall. Quinquefolia is the clue. Just remember that Virginia creeper has five leaflets and poison ivy has three, and you'll never confuse this most desirable of wild vines with that vicious weed.

Like its relative, Boston ivy, Virginia creeper will climb brick or stone walls, trail along the ground, or clamber over brush or shrubs without strangling them. It is a vigorous grower with large leaves, a

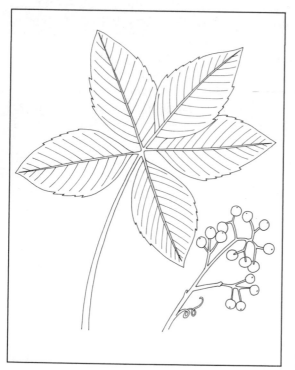

Virginia Creeper

fact to bear in mind on a small property unless you have something it can climb. All in all, it is one of the best of our native vines, easy to transplant, with no special requirements. It will grow in shade as well as sun, but the fall coloring won't be as flamboyant. It's also an excellent plant for attracting birds since it provides cover and nesting as well as good food.

WILD CLEMATIS (Virgin's Bower, Love Vine, Woodbine)
Clematis

There are nearly three hundred species of wild clematis, and many of them are native to North America. One most often offered by dealers is *C. paniculata* which produces clouds of tiny white flowers in late summer. Clematis has no bad habits and is beautifully suited to the sunny wild garden. Try it near a wall or in the wild area along a road.

For further reading:
Gardening in the Shade, Brooklyn Botanic Garden, 1000 Washington Ave., Brooklyn, N.Y. 11225.
Ground Cover Plants, Donald Wyman, Macmillan, New York, 1956.
The Complete Shade Gardener, George Schenk, Houghton Mifflin, Boston, 1984

CHAPTER 4

Ferns

Our native ferns are among the hardiest, most versatile, and most widely available of all wild plants. Although no one would design a woodland garden without them, we don't begin to take advantage of the variety of ways they can be used in the home landscape. Except in the desert, there are ferns to suit virtually every site—some are rugged enough to survive even a polluted city environment—and a properly placed fern, or even a "green" garden composed solely of ferns, provides us with a sense of serene beauty that few flowering plants can equal.

Perhaps "properly placed" is the clue to why ferns aren't more popular with modern gardeners. In the old, gone-to-seed garden we acquired with our last house, the sunny perennial beds were overrun with ferns, crowding out the flowers, and shabby from too much sun. Many of us, I suspect, think of ferns in the garden in terms of neglect, in a class with the dusty Boston fern of the Victorian parlor.

With the exception of the hay-scented fern and one or two others that tolerate sun, ferns belong in shade, even the deep shade where

ABOVE: Hosta, epimedium, and evergreen euonymous edge a planting of royal fern, cinnamon fern, and false Solomon's seal. *(George Taloumis)*

flowering plants won't grow. If you take advantage of this need for shade, along with their habit of growth—slowly unfurling fiddleheads that open just when the early spring flowers and bulbs have finished their bloom, leaving yellowing, ripening foliage and then bare spots— you can see why ferns are such useful garden plants. Try them among the bulbs you grow under deciduous trees, where the summer shade makes it impractical to interplant your bulbs with annuals. Ferns have other advantages over annuals too, if easy-maintenance gardening is what you are seeking; they are permanent and don't have to be bought and planted each year. And as they grow they act as a ground cover to conserve moisture and prevent the growth of weeds.

Ferns add textural interest to a foundation planting, especially when mixed with other wild or cultivated ground covers. Combine them with wild blue phlox or Virginia bluebells, violets, lilies-of-the-valley, even that old standby, pachysandra. Or plant them behind an edging of ajuga for a handsome, no-care contrast of color and texture.

If you have a border bed of trees and shrubs along the back or sides of your property, underplant it with ferns, including the spreading or so-called invasive ones, and you'll never have to weed again.

In the shady rock garden, try the tough little rock-cap fern, which is easy to establish, indestructible, and evergreen.

One handsome fern at the corner of a building or beside a pair of steps can do as much for your landscape design as the traditional spreading yew, and at far less cost. We never could get anything to grow at the front corner of our garage because of the downspout from the roof. A few years ago, we put in a sensitive fern (so named because it dies back at the first frost, although no earlier, I find, than any other deciduous plant) in that spot. It completely solved our problem of constant erosion and turned an eyesore into a most attractive land- scape accent. Since the fern is spreading, or "invasive," I do have to break a piece off every now and then to keep it under control, but this is really no trouble, and provides me with new plants to use elsewhere.

In most articles about ferns you will find a warning to keep invasive ferns out of the garden. Yet if you have a rough bank or any area where you need a fast-growing ground cover, an invasive fern may be exactly what you need. The answer is not in avoiding all invasive ferns, but in using the right fern in the right place. (Actually, this may be where I should admit that I am not one of those gardeners for whom every green thing grows and flourishes, which may be one reason why I am often grateful to the pretty plant that someone else complains of as being rampant. Usually what is invasive to others is just a strong grower for me. Besides, if a plant I like happens to do very well, that means I can have more of it by division or new seedlings.)

Ferns not only look cool, they actually do provide coolness and conserve moisture for the plants around and beneath them. In a new wildflower garden, you may not yet have enough shade for some of the more delicate wildflowers. But if you plant ferns with them, you will find that they will shelter the delicate hepatica, shortia, and even trailing arbutus while they are getting established, and at the same time create an "instant" woodland effect. Similarly, new plantings of rhododendron, azaleas, and holly need to have their roots protected from the summer's heat. Because ferns are generally surface growers, they act as a permanent, living mulch.

FERN CULTURE

The ferns described at the end of this chapter, except for some of those marked "difficult," are not rare and may therefore be collected from the wild or purchased. Please read the chapter on collecting and conservation and, as with all flowers, obey the rules about leaving roadside plantings intact for others to enjoy.

In general, ferns want rich, moist, woodsy soil; even those that grow naturally in sun or in dry or rocky earth need moisture and shade for a good start. If your soil is naturally thin and sandy, or heavy with clay, any generous combination of humus, compost, leaf mold, and peat moss will improve it. Even if your soil is rich to start with, it is a good idea to add compost or other organic matter every time you dig a hold for a new plant.

More ferns die from being planted too deep than from not being planted deep enough, so you should note whether your fern grows from a crown or from a running rootstock. Plant the crown-rooted fern in a shallow, saucer-shaped hole, large enough to let you spread out the roots and just deep enough so that the tip of the crown is barely above the surface. This is slightly deeper than you would have found it growing wild. If your soil needs improving, make the hole deeper, fill it with good, rich earth, and then set the crown in place. Cover the roots with soil, and water well. Mulch. Ferns that grow from running creeping rootstock should be planted an inch or so below ground level. Otherwise, the planting procedure is the same.

After your ferns have been planted and watered, mulch them heavily. A thick layer of porous mulch not only protects new plantings from drying out, and old ones from drought or extremes of temperature; it eventually decomposes and adds to the organic matter of the soil itself. Mulching is the best garden labor-saving device I know. Besides eliminating or cutting down the chores of weeding, watering, and fertilizing it, can save you the trouble of raking up and carting away garden debris. In areas where the mulching won't show, or appearance doesn't matter, you can even skip the intermediate step of making a compost or leaf-mold pile—just put the raw materials, the weeds or grass clippings or leaves (but not heavy, soggy maple leaves) right where you want them.

The best time to transplant ferns is in early spring or in the fall, but you can really move them at any time if you observe the usual precautions against transplanting on a hot sunny day and against keeping them out of the earth any longer than is absolutely necessary. When you move full-grown ferns, cut back some of the fronds. When you dig them up, don't help them out of the ground by tugging on the fronds; they'll just break off. However, if some do break in the process, don't despair, new ones will grow.

There are well over a hundred species of ferns in this country, with innumerable subspecies and variations of interest only to an expert. If you collect your ferns from the wild and make sure to plant your specimens in a similar environment at home, you don't really have to know their names, although you'll no doubt become interested enough after a while to invest in a fern guide to find out what you have.

If you buy your ferns, on the other hand, you really do need to know the names and habits of those most commonly offered, since difficult-to-grow specimens are rarely so identified by the man who wants to sell them, and invasive varieties are usually tabbed with a euphemism like "strong grower," if they are identified at all. Moreover, quite a few of the most popular ferns look almost identical to the amateur eye, making it easy to order what sounds like a varied collection of ferns only to discover that they all look alike.

Since fern heights are extremely variable, even in nature, but especially when you compare a fern in its native environment with its twin in a garden, I do not include in the descriptions below any specific information about fern heights. (A six-foot fern may reach a maximum height of three feet, or even less, under cultivation.) Instead, the ferns below are classified into three groups: monarchs, intermediates, and miniatures.

THE MONARCHS

CINNAMON FERN
Osmunda cinnamonea

INTERRUPTED FERN
O. claytoniana

ROYAL FERN
O. regalis

All are stately plants that like a moist, acid, woodsy soil. They are crown-formers and will not spread, which makes them extremely useful for places where you want one dramatic accent. Give them plenty of rich soil, and mulch heavily with oak leaves or other acid-supplying material. If there is enough moisture, all three of these Osmundas can stand quite a bit of sun.

Osmunda regalis

Cinnamon Fern gets its name from its separate stalks with brown spore cases; you'll have no trouble identifying this one.

Interrupted Fern is just as aptly named; the fertile fronds are interrupted part way down, where pairs of small leaflets carrying the spores are located. These fertile leaflets wither early in summer, making the interrupted effect most noticeable.

Royal Fern, although it has the same habits as the other two, doesn't look very much like a fern at all. It leaves look more like those of a locust tree, with little leaflets at the tips that contain the spores, and look enough like incipient flowers to account for the royal's other common name, flowering fern.

OSTRICH FERN
Pteretis nodulosa

This fourth monarch fern is tall and stately, with plume-shaped fronds that grow in a vaselike manner. Although it, too, is a crown-forming plant, it does spread rapidly from underground runners if it is planted in its ideal environment, wet shade. It's a good choice to control erosion along the banks of a stream or in a wet, marshy spot. In dry shade, however, it won't spread very much and makes a handsome background plant in a shady garden spot.

THE INTERMEDIATES

This group contains the best and most generally useful ferns for the garden. It also contains most of the spreading, or invasive, ferns.

MAIDENHAIR FERN
Adiantum pedatum

This is everybody's favorite, with its delicate palmate leaves atop wiry black stems. Although it spreads, no one would call it invasive, and it is a lovely filler for bulbs and other spring-flowering woodland plants. It needs a deeply mulched woodsy soil, shade, good drainage, and moisture. In spite of its delicate appearance, no one but me seems to find it anything but very easy to grow, and I shall continue to try.

CHRISTMAS FERN
Polystichum acrostichoides

This is another extremely popular fern and is fully evergreen no matter how cold the winters. It also spreads, again not invasively, a fact I

Polystichum acrostichoides

know only because I've read it. My own observation, in the woods or a garden, is that the Christmas fern always appears as a separate plant. No matter, it's very handsome, thrives in deep shade and, although it likes moisture, will tolerate quite dry conditions. In the garden, this makes it an excellent choice under hemlocks or other evergreen trees.

WOODFERNS OR SHIELD FERNS

These ferns are confusing because each of them is known by a number of common names, and because they look almost identical anyway. The best thing to do is to concentrate on the botanical name, *Dryopteris*; then, no matter what they are called in the catalog, you'll know how many of this particular type you are buying.

Dryopteris marginalis (marginal woodfern, evergreen woodfern, leather-leaf woodfern, marginal shield fern) is fully evergreen. Its deep blue-green fronds grow in a vase, or shield, from a crown root.

Dryopteris spinulosa or *D. intermedia* (spinulose woodfern, toothed woodfern, or fancy fern) is slightly less evergreen than *D. marginalis*, but otherwise virtually identical.

Either of these ferns, by whatever name, is good in a typical woodland setting or in any shady border as an accent plant. They need shade, but otherwise are undemanding.

The following ferns are "invasive"; consider them when you need a fast-growing ground cover, particularly in a problem area.

HAY-SCENTED FERN
Dennstaedtia punctilobula

This fern grows well in sun or light shade, and also on rocky outcroppings. It's a good ground cover for open banks and thrives in good or poor soil. It has feathery light green fronds that look lovely with flowers and last very well in the house.

LADY FERN
Athyrium filix-femina

This delicate-looking light green fern needs shade and moisture or it gets to look shabby.

Athyrium filiy temina

NEW YORK FERN
Thelypteris noveboracensis

Feathery and delicate in appearance, this fern is somewhat taller than the previous two. Since it is one of the first ferns to turn brown in the fall, it is less desirable.

SENSITIVE FERN
Onoclea sensibilis

With broader fronds than any of the ferns mentioned so far, Sensitive Fern is described as handsome and showy by those who like it, as I do, and coarse by those who don't. In a fairly dry garden, it doesn't spread very fast, but it does reseed itself all summer, supplying you with lots of little plants to move to other places or to leave alone if you are using it as a ground cover. Unlike most other ferns though, its separate stalks of spore cases last all winter; they are attractive additions to dried-flower arrangements.

BRACKEN
Pteridium aquilinum

This three-part fern has fronds that spread horizontally to the ground atop a tallish stalk. You see it in thickets, along dry roadsides in sun or shade, in neglected areas, and in poor soil. It isn't a choice garden fern, but if you have a roadside or a large area that supports little else but weeds, bracken is surely a better alternative.

THE MINIATURES

Although there are lots of little ferns, and many are offered by wild-flower dealers, most of them are in the difficult category and not for beginners. These four are easy:

OAK FERN
Dryopteris Linnaeana (sometimes called Gymnocarpium dryopteris)

Oak fern looks like a miniature, light green version of bracken, but delicate and charming. It creeps, but not invasively, and makes a lovely ground cover in a moist, shady woodland garden.

The strong lines of sensitive fern provide contrast to pachysandra under an evergreen border planting. *(Author)*

COMMON POLYPODY (Rock-cap Fern)
Polypodium vulgare

This small, dark, evergreen fern is often found imbedded in moss. It can cover huge rocks in sheets. It is extremely easy to grow and to transplant; simply break off a piece of the moss and plant it—don't try to extricate the matted roots or pull it out by the roots if you find it growing on a rock without the moss.

Although polypody is easy to grow in rock crevices, give it some soil to start with; either plant it next to a rock and let it find its own way into the crevices, or put some leaf-mold in the crevice and then anchor your transplant down with a weight until it gets established. Be sure to break off a few pieces in fall to bring inside. Its small size and neat growth make polypody ideal for a terrarium.

LITTLE GRAY POLYPODY (Resurrection Fern)
Polypodium polypodioides

Similar to the rock-cap fern, it is native to the South where it climbs on trees and dead branches instead of rocks. Its nickname derives from the fact that it curls up and appears dead in dry weather, but revives and turns green again as soon as it gets some moisture.

EBONY SPLEENWORT
Asplenium platyneuron

This one looks like a miniature evergreen Christmas fern, and what could be nicer? It likes shade and moisture, but will even stand sun if it doesn't dry out. It looks particularly handsome next to a rock or a gnarled root, and like the polypodies, it is a natural choice for a shady rock garden.

The following ferns, although offered for sale by most wildflower dealers, are generally regarded as difficult plants:

Maidenhair Spleenwort, *Asplenium Trichomanes*

Walking Fern, *Camptosorus rhizophyllus*

Hartford Climbing Fern, *Lygodium palmatum*

All of the Grape Ferns, *Botrichium*, including Rattlesnake Fern *Botrichium virginianum*

The Chain Ferns, *Woodwardia*

Fern Check Lists

Evergreen ferns:
Christmas Fern
Common Polypody
Resurrection Fern
Marginal Woodfern
Ebony Spleenwort

Ferns that will tolerate sun:
Cinnamon Fern
Interrupted Fern
Royal Fern
Hay-scented Fern

Ferns for a city garden:
Hay-scented Fern
Cinnamon Fern
Christmas Fern
Common Polypody

For further reading:

Handbook on Ferns, Brooklyn Botanic Garden, 1000 Washington Ave., Brooklyn, N. Y. 11225.

Ferns to Know and Grow, F. Gordon Foster, Hawthorn, N. Y., 1971.

A Field Guide to the Ferns and Their Related Families of Northeastern and Central North America, Boughton Cobb (Peterson Field Guide Series), Houghton Mifflin, Boston, 1968.

CHAPTER 5

The Woodland Garden

When I was a child growing up in a New York City suburb, one of the delights of spring was walking in a nearby woods. With no premonition that this could become a rare experience, we indiscriminately enjoyed violets, skunk cabbages, fiddleheads, and pink lady slippers. I often pass that spot today, but it exists only in my memory and, appropriately engraved in stone, as part of the name of the subdivision that replaced it. None of the original trees, no wildflowers, not even the streams that crisscrossed our paths remain. I don't know what happened to the little pond in a clearing where we watched with endless fascination the polliwogs as they grew up into frogs. Perhaps the water was diverted into a concrete conduit.

Although that woods would be no safer from development today, one hopes that it might have a slightly better chance of surviving such total obliteration. Belatedly, some builders are realizing the importance, or at least the sales value, of leaving wooded land in some sort

ABOVE: Great snow trillium among English Ivy and myrtle. *(George Taloumis)*

of close-to-natural state. And homeowners, who once would have seen no alternative to lawns and flower beds, are now beginning to think more and more in terms of preserving even a small piece of woodland— sometimes out of love of nature, sometimes out of dislike for the chore of mowing a lawn.

For whichever reason, if you are lucky enough to have a wooded area on your land, or if you own an entirely wooded piece of property, the second half of this chapter will help you preserve it, plant it, even improve it.

But without the advantage of a natural piece of woods, or even so much as a single tree, you can still have a woodland garden, provided you live in an area where there is enough rainfall to support trees. Actually, you can grow the woodland plants without trees, in the shade of a lathe house or a north wall of a building, but this is not quite the same as a woodland garden. To paraphrase the saying that you can't see the woods for the trees, it is just as true that you can't have a woods without trees.

THE SOIL

In chapter two, we talked about the wildflowers you can grow in a shady garden bed. Virtually all of these may also be grown in a woodland wildflower garden. On the other hand, there is a whole range of shade flowers that simply will not thrive in your ordinary garden bed. These denizens of the forest rquire "woodsy" soil, a word you will repeatedly come across in books and articles on wildflower gardening. Without this woodsy soil, the plant you most carefully dig up from the forest will eventually sicken and die in your garden. With proper soil, you may find it surprisingly easy to grow even rare and temperamental beauties of the woods.

Woodsy soil is that marvelously springy, spongy material you feel under your feet when you walk through a forest. If you poke your fingers down into it, you will find that beneath the topmost layer of leaves or evergreen needles are succeeding layers—although with no perceptible divisions—of the same material, each a little more decomposed than the one above, until the last layer is totally crumbled. If your woods is near a beach, you may be surprised to come upon pure white sand beneath the woodsy soil. If you do, you may well find trailing arbutus and pink lady slippers in the vicinity. But look only, don't touch! Both of these, like most other woodland plants, are on protected lists everywhere. If you even pick the lady slipper, the plant will die.

This top forest layer of decayed and decaying vegetable matter is *humus*, the organic portion of soil. Garden loam, or topsoil, is composed of a mixture of organic humus and inorganic mineral soil, the sand or clay that is derived from rock. Sand or clay subsoil contains no humus.

One of the several important qualities of humus, beyond enriching the soil and providing an environment for microscopic organisms necessary for growth, is its ability to hold water. According to Taylor's *Encyclopedia of Gardening*, mineral subsoil can absorb only about twenty per cent of its own weight in water; good garden topsoil may hold as much as sixty per cent of its weight, but forest humus can absorb from 300 to 500 per cent of its weight in water!

If you are a new homeowner and don't know what kind of soil you have, or what the builder has left behind, look at your land right after a rain. If the water has disappeared and the surface dries out quickly, your soil is sandy. If the water remains standing in puddles, your soil is basically clay. But if the water is absorbed and the ground remains moist, you are probably blessed with a pretty good layer of topsoil.

Although woodsy soil is essential to the success of a woodland wildflower garden, it is not difficult to get, or make, or even imitate. Moreover, many woodland flowers are shallow-rooted and actually grow above "ground" in the top layer of humus. This means that you don't have to dig out a woodland wildflower bed to the ideal eighteen or twenty-four inches, but can get away with as little as six inches of over-all preparation, with an occasional deeper hole which you can dig later for individual plants. Once established, the depth of your forest floor will be increased from the top by natural leaf-fall, and if you give nature a hand by regular generous top dressings of compost, humus, or any organic mulch, you can build up the humus layer over the years instead of the centuries.

PREPARING THE WOODLAND SOIL

A working formula for woodsy soil is:

  1 part sharp builder's sand (not beach sand)
  1 part garden loam
  3 parts acid peat moss*
    (*see descriptions of peat moss below)

This is a useful prescription if you are going to make your garden on a penthouse terrace, in a container, or on a very small scale. However, it strkes me unnecessarily expensive for the average gardener except, perhaps, for one so obsessively neat that he hasn't allowed a leaf, a twig, or a blade of grass to remain on the ground.

In general, the way to turn garden soil into woodsy soil is simply to incorporate large—and I do mean large—amount of any and all kinds of vegetable humus into your own variety of garden dirt. If you are preparing your bed during spring and fall clean-up time, simply take everything you rake up off the lawn and out of the beds and add it to your prospective wildflower bed. If you have a compost heap, a leaf-mold pile, or the jumble of both I couldn't be without, this is the time and place to use it all up. None of this material needs to be thoroughly decomposed; in fact, it will be even better if it isn't, since a good forest floor contains material in all stages of decomposition. When you get into the spirit of this thing, you may find woodland ingredients in unexpected places. One day my husband and I were visiting a friend who complained that her garden had been so neglected the previous year when they were away that the pine needles were killing her lawn. Since, as it happened, we had large plastic leaf bags in the car, we came away with a magnificent supply of beautiful forest mulch. Another time two little girls, whose family had just moved into the house behind ours, watched with puzzlement as I stood crumbling a rotted piece of wood and scattering it over the wildflower garden. When I explained what I was doing, they told me their father had just finished cleaning up their backyard, separating the good fire wood from the rotten stuff, and would I like to have the latter? Naturally, I insisted they ask permission first (and who knows what kind of eccentric their family thought they had as a neighbor?)—but I acquired a lot of beautiful rotted wood, along with two charming helpers who had a great time crumbling and spreading it around. The larger pieces of still-intact logs we simply left on the bed. Gradually, as in any real woods, they will rot away; meanwhile they make attractive backgrounds for ferns, trilliums, and other wildflowers that like to grow near a congenial rotting log.

If cleaning up your own place and scavenging doesn't provide you with enough forest soil, peat moss will do very well. In either case, if your own garden dirt is very heavy, you might also want to use some sand. On the other hand, if your soil is very sandy, you don't have to add clay, just an extra-generous helping of organic material. In fact, if you want to, and you have enough compost (which has soil mixed in it), you can remove all of the original soil and make a woodland garden bed out of nothing but compost and other organic material.

As you can see, there is no one right formula for making a woodland flower bed. The important thing is to understand what it is you are trying to imitate and then duplicate it in whatever way you can. However, no matter what you incorporate into your bed, it is necessary to let it settle for a time before setting out your plants. This can be a matter of days or weeks if you are using the loam-peat-moss-sand formula, but if you have used a lot of rough, undecayed material, such as pieces of logs and freshly raked leaves, you had better let the bed settle over the winter.

(The above is a case of do as I say, not what I do. I myself was much too impatient to let my woodland garden settle before I began to plant a few ferns, lilies-of-the-valley, and other fairly rugged plants. I did make sure, though, that their roots were in contact with some soil, not air pockets or undecomposed material, and they don't seem the worse for my impatience.)

ACID-SOIL REQUIREMENTS OF WOODLAND PLANTS

Woodland wildflowers grow in soil that ranges from neutral to very acid, which brings us to the question of how you measure the pH (hydrogen ion) factor in your soil. How do you tell whether it is alkaline, neutral, slightly acid, moderately acid, or very acid? It also raises the question of how important the pH factor is to the gardener-hobbyist. There is no consensus on this second point; opinions range from those who hold that wildflowers must be grown in soil of exactly the correct acidity, to people like the owners of Orchid Gardens Nursery who state that in their forty years of growing wildflowers for sale they have never bothered about the acid requirements of their plants, and consider such other factors as shade, humus, water, and air much more significant.

It is fair to assume that the people at Orchid Gardens do have soil of the approximately correct acidity or they wouldn't be in that business. If you want to be accurate and don't mind the trouble, you can buy a pH measuring kit or send soil samples to your county agricultural agent. If you do either of these, though, be sure to do it right. With a trowel, dig up a sample of dirt ten inches deep, mix it up well, and then take a sample from the mixed-up dirt. You do this because soil is more acid at the top, where the organic matter is relatively undecomposed, than it is lower down. The other thing to remember is that you want to take samples from various parts of your garden (or at least from those parts where you intend to plant wildflowers). The soil under an oak tree, for example, will be far more acid than that in a rose bed on the other side of your house. Be sure to label carefully the location of each sample.

For myself, frankly, I must admit that when gardening begins to sound like a chemistry assignment, my enthusiasm wanes perceptibly. It wasn't pure concern for the environment that made me so happy to give up insecticides, fungicides, and chemical fertilizers, or even all the work of spreading and spraying; it was also relief at not having to figure out strengths, proportions, coverages, and other incomprehensible data.

Fortunately, it doesn't have to be so complicated, so if the class will give me its attention for a few minutes, we will see how you can learn to tell by observation what plants you can expect to grow and where. First, to master the pH scale:

The pH scale runs from 1 to 14—pH 7 is neutral; any number below 7 is acid; any number above 7 is alkaline. Plants grow within the 4-to-9 range, and very few exist at either extreme.

If you don't want to memorize the numbers below, you don't have to. They are included here because you may run across them elsewhere.

Translated into the generally used terms:

pH 9 = very alkaline	pH 6 = slightly acid
pH 8 = alkaline	pH 5 = moderately acid
pH 7 = neutral	pH 4 = very acid

The range of acidity or alkalinity indicated by these numbers is greater than you may think, since the difference between any two adjacent numbers represents a multiple of ten. In other words, soil with a pH of 6 is ten times more acid than pH 7 (neutral) soil: pH 5 is one hundred times more acid, and pH 4 is a thousand times more acid, than pH7.

Sometimes you will see pH numbers carried to a decimal point. If you do, just ignore it and use the nearest whole number. Thus, pH 6.8 may be read as pH 7. pH 6.5 may be read as pH 6–7.

The fact of the matter is that most plants show a considerable tolerance when it comes to the degree of acidity or alkalinity under which they will grow.

Most vegetables and flowers, including wildflowers, will grow in soils ranging from pH 6 to pH 8. Most woodland wildflowers will grow in the pH 6-to-7 range. Since this happens to be the range within which most garden topsoil falls, you can see why many people don't worry about the pH content of their soils.

Nevertheless, since woodland plants are rather fussier than most (or at least some of them are), it is useful to know what you can grow, and where, and how you can change and improve your soil if you want to.

Generally speaking, alkaline soils occur in heavily limestone areas, some western deserts, salt marshes, and the dunes right at the seashore (not behind it). Within these delineations, however, there are many exceptions. You may even find considerable variation on a suburban quarter-acre—you could have alkaline soil against the concrete foundation of the house, acid soil under a hemlock hedge or a foundation planting of rhododendrons, neutral soil in the flower bed, and slightly acid soil on the lawns.

Repeated applications of chemical fertilizers tend to make soil acid. In the eastern states and other naturally acid areas, gardeners counteract this overacidity by periodic applications of agricultural limestone. Of course, only lawns and flower or vegetable beds should be limed, not an azalea-rhododendron foundation planting. So without taking actual measurements, you can pretty well judge the acidity of your soil by observation. If you have hemlocks, pines or oak trees and are successful with rhododendrons, laurel, azaleas, and dogwood, your soil, in those areas at least, will support most woodland plants without increasing the acidity.

If your soil is not acid enough, but you have adequate shade and water and can provide the woodsy humus described earlier, you can increase the acidity of your woodland garden rather easily. (Actually, it is possible to turn a patch of alkaline soil into acid soil for a wildflower bed, but this is a never-ending project and not one to be recommended to anyone interested in natural gardening.)

The easiest way to increase acidity in a bed is by adding large quantities of *acid* peat moss to the soil as you prepare it, by continuing to add more of this material as you dig planting holes, and by periodic top dressing with acid material: oak leaves, pine needles, or more acid peat. If you also plant oak trees, pines, or other natural producers of acid leafmold, they will take over the job for you.

All peat moss is not the same. Without becoming too involved in the complexities here, garden peat moss comes basically from two sources—the forest floor, where it is derived from decomposed leaves, twigs, trees, and shrubs, and is usually sold as leaf mold or humus; and from the sphagnum mosses that grow in bogs. Acid peat moss is untreated sphagnum moss from the bogs.

The rougher your peat moss and the lighter in color, the more acid it will be. Michigan and Pennsylvania peat, fine in texture and dark in color, have a pH of 6. They are not acid enough to change the chemistry of your soil, although they are excellent conditioners for lawns, flower beds, and woodland gardens that are already sufficiently acid. The very fine, expensive, almost black humus, also sold in bags, is thoroughly decomposed organic material and tests neutral on the pH scale.

Similarly, if you use your own compost instead of peat moss, bear in mind that it, too, will show variations of acidity depending on what you put into it, but also on the state of decomposition. Partially decomposed material will be more acid than fine dark, totally decomposed material that has achieved the stage known as humus and looks like good black topsoil.

The only other thing to remember about increasing the acidity of your soil is that it takes a *lot* of acid material to change the pH factor appreciably. As you remember, soil with a pH factor of 5 is 100 times as acid as neutral soil (pH 7).

Too much acidity is rarely a problem in a woodland garden. If you have the rare soil that is too acid, correct it by incorporating loam from another part of your garden, thoroughly decomposed compost, or Michigan or Pennsylvania peat into your beds, and be sure not to use acid-producing mulches. In general, you are better off not trying to decrease appreciably the acidity of your woodland garden soil, since there is probably a natural reason why it is acid in the first place (such as the presence of oak trees or evergreens). Instead, why not take advantage of the acid soil to grow the very beautiful wildflowers that either demand or tolerate very acid conditions. You will find some of these at the end of the chapter as well as in the chapter on ground covers.

WATER

Even though your woodsy soil has remarkable water-retention qualities, even though the presence of trees provides a humid atmosphere, and even though many woodland plants grow naturally in a dry woods, you must locate your flower bed where you can bring in plenty of water for at least the first few years. After that, if you live in a section of the country where rainfall is plentiful, your garden should get along with little or no extra watering from you.

But meanwhile, if watering is going to mean a daily bout with a long hose, you aren't going to enjoy it. Although we tend to equate shade with moisture, since dirt in the sun dries out much faster than dirt in the shade, it is a mistake to think the soil under a large tree, especially one with shallow roots, will retain sufficient moisture. Much of the rain never even penetrates the leafy canopy of the trees, and the water that does is quickly absorbed by the tree roots. The earth beneath the trees may dry out without your even noticing it.

Similarly, unless the trees in your woodland garden are very high-branched, water from a sprinkler set outside the garden itself will wet down the outer branches of the trees and run off, again without penetrating the earth under the trees.

Unless you have a natural source of water, such as a brook or a stream, or an underground watering system, an easy way to bring water to your garden is to set a sprinkler right in the garden and leave it there. Then replace your outdoor water faucet with a double (or triple) faucet attachment and leave one hose permanently connected to one of the faucet heads for the exclusive purpose of watering the woodland garden.

To avoid the unsightly appearance of a hose strung across the grounds from faucet to sprinkler, buy lightweight plastic hose, which is not affected by freezing, and lay it under the sod. Since you don't have to dig a deep trench, this is a relatively easy job: simply take a sharp spade, slice into the sod on a slant, lay the hose in the cut, and replace the grass. You will hardly know the lawn has been disturbed. When you select a sprinkler, try to get one that will cover your bed completely, so you don't have to move it around. With this permanently attached hose, watering your woodland garden is no more difficult than turning on the faucet. With a multiple faucet head, you won't even have to unscrew the hose when you want to water other parts of your garden.

Above and beyond what it does for the plants, water in the woodland garden makes everything look and smell like a new spring day. Moving water attracts birds, so if you add a bird bath, you can water the plants, fill the bath, and attract the birds with one turn of the faucet. What more could you ask?

* * *

LOCATING THE GARDEN

Although it is perfectly possible to grow woodland wildflowers in the shade of an object other than a tree, I think it is foolish to pretend you can create a woodland garden without trees. Please note the plural; one tree in the middle of a lawn is not a woods. On the other hand, if your one tree is located in an area that would be suited for a little woods, you can bring in other, smaller trees to augment it.

As a rule, the middle of a lawn is not a good place anyway for a woodland garden. If you recall your last walk in the woods, one of the qualities you noted, subconsciously perhaps, was the sense of stillness and quiet; if there was a wind, you felt it only as a presence high in the trees, not on the ground. Keep this in mind when you lay out your garden, and don't place it out in the open where the delicate plants will be subject to hot winds or driving rains. The plants actually need less protection against the cold of winter than against the hot drying winds of summer, especially winds that heat up as they pass over asphalt or concrete. So from both the esthetic and horticultural points of view, a garden placed against a background planting of trees and shrubs, or even near a protective fence, will do better and look more natural than one in the open.

If you have no trees at all, you have, oddly enough, a double advantage: you can locate your garden wherever you like and you can select the trees most suitable for a little woods. Needless to say, your woods won't spring up overnight, but you can get a start while the trees are still small.

The easiest way to begin is to lay out your bed and prepare your soil before you plant the trees, rather than planting trees and then having to dig up around them. Although it is not possible to prescribe the best trees for every section of the country, keep certain facts in mind when selecting trees:

1. Little trees grow up. Don't plant them too close together; instead rely on shrubs or naturally smaller trees to supply you with a windbreak or screening.

2. Don't plant a solid stand of the same trees of the same age and size. As they grow to maturity, they will either grow spindly or, as in the case of white pines, they will all lose their lower branches as they reach for the sun.

3. Select trees that are deep-rooted (avoid maples and elms) and that will provide the acid leafmold that your garden needs. Oak trees

and pines or other evergreens are excellent for this purpose. A clump of white birch is effective against the dark evergreens. Dogwood is ideal; it is beautiful in itself, combines well with wildflowers and, because it is deciduous yet has spreading branches, lets the sun filter through in spring while providing plenty of shade in summer.

Once again, however, if you are starting from scratch, you should consult a book on trees or a good local nurseryman. In addition, look at the trees that grow *naturally* in your area, as opposed to the specimens that your neighbors may have planted. (A rather poor source of information is the roadside nursery stand; like many of their plants, their trees were probably imported from other parts of the country. While they may be just what you need, then again, they may not.)

Native shrubs, such as rhododendron, deciduous azaleas, mountain laurel, and Oregon holly, are beautiful background plants for a woodland garden and essential to one that does not already have mature trees.

After you plant your trees and shrubs, set out a few of the larger ferns, since these too will provide shade for the smaller, more delicate wildflowers. They will also give you almost immediately the illusion of a woodland. If you watch the shade patterns made by this beginning of a woods, you can start right in with a few of the easier wildflowers, or the little ones you can tuck in the shadow of a fern or against the trunk of a tree. It may seem only a small beginning, but have you ever noticed how beautiful even one hepatica looks against a tree trunk in earliest spring?

On an already landscaped property, it isn't always possible to find the ideal site for a woodland garden. Yet with some trimming and changing (and even cheating) you can usually find a border or a bed that you can transform into a small wildwood. On our fairly typical suburban one-third acre, a spindly privet hedge under a row of large hemlocks screened us from our neighbor to the rear. The hemlock branches, which had never been pruned, hung to the ground. This gave us great privacy but over the years, as they encroached farther and farther over our lawn, made the back yard seem smaller and smaller. Needless to say, nothing at all flourished under their boughs.

Although we were reluctant to lose privacy by limbing up the trees, when we finally took the step, we made a number of pleasant discoveries: the back yard seemed twice as big, the privet hedge grew taller and thicker in the added light, and we also had room for more interesting background shrubs. Best of all, we had a brand-new fifty-foot bed to fill with wildflowers. Admittedly, with no deciduous trees to let in the spring sunshine, it is still shadier than even a woodland garden ought to be, but ferns do well toward the back and we are now successfully growing trillium, trout lilies, Virginia bluebells, violets, galax, forget-me-nots (in a wettish spot), May apples, lilies-of-the-valley, and half a dozen other wildflowers in a place where even mere pachysandra was unable to survive before.

The really ideal location for a woodland garden on our property was even worse, so far as growing anything was concerned. This was at the point where the back and side borders joined. Here we had a pink dogwood growing beneath an ancient maple tree. From the maple to the back and side boundaries of our land, virtually nothing would grow, and what did was hidden when the dogwood leaves came out. Drastic pruning of the maple and judicious limbing up of the dogwood let in light and gave the dogwood a new lease on life. But it was literally impossible to dig a hole, much less a flower bed, into earth that held an impenetrable mass of tree-trunk-sized maple roots.

What if we built a bed above the ground, using rocks to hold the fill, but sloping down toward the rear and side borders, so as to avoid the formal appearance of a raised rock garden? It was all very unscientific and in retrospect a real rock garden was probably called for. In the frame of that landscape design, however, it still seems to me that a real rock garden would have been out of place. Anyway, we felt we had nothing to lose. Besides, the compost piles were getting out of hand, and this would be an excellent way to clean them out completely, using *all* of the material in whatever stage of decomposition. With that rationalization, we hauled in everything we could lay our hands on: logs and kindling too rotten to burn, discarded tree branches, extra dirt and sand from other gardening projects, even stones and pieces of brick. As the bed built up, we threw in more rocks to hold the dirt, keeping the new soil a foot or two away from the tree trunks in order not to injure the trees. The roughest compost and the freshly raked leaves went in too, but as we approached the top level, we mixed the old, fine compost with a few bales of peat moss. Properly, all of this should have been allowed to settle at least over the winter, but I was impatient and started right in by transplanting ferns, violets, seedling evergreens that had sprouted near their parents, and a few other hardy plants from other parts of the garden. As the fall and winter progressed, we threw evergreen prunings and discarded Christmas tree branches over the bed. By spring, their needles had dropped and it was an easy matter to remove the unsightly bare branches.

The big question, of course, was whether the roots of the maple tree, given such a lush new environment, would take over before the wild plants could become established. Once wildflowers *are* established, they don't seem to mind tree roots; in fact appear to like growing amongst them. It has been five years now and the garden is doing better each year. The plants that did well from the beginning—trailing arbutus, partridgeberry, shortia, bloodroot, trillium, Jack-in-the-pulpit, hepatica, wild ginger, galax, and lots of ferns and violets—are flourishing. The flowers that should never have been put there in the first place, such as shooting star, May apple, and Dutchman's breeches, all of which prefer less acid soil and more sun, died out right away.

This, by the way, is one of the big differences between wildflowers and cultivated plants. The latter, being more adaptable to a wider range of growing conditions, will live on, albeit in a sickly state, if they don't have optimum conditions—which usually means that a gardener spends a lot of time nursing plants he'd be better off without. Even though some woodland wildflowers are slow in getting started, especially those that are dug up from the wild, in general they'll either love you or leave you and not just hang around for years putting out weak little blossoms to get you to baby them for one more year.

I don't mean to imply from this that you should never try again if once you've failed with a plant, as long as you really want it and have reason to believe it ought to grow for you. Sometimes just a few feet in one direction or another makes the difference. On your second attempt, try three specimens of the same plant in three different spots, and if it does well in any one of them, put future specimens there.

THE WOODLAND PATH

Unless your garden is so tiny that you can reach every corner of it without trampling over the porous soil, you need some kind of path. In a very small bed, a few stepping stones will serve. However, any woods needs a path to give perspective and to allow you to get close enough to appreciate the very small flowers. There are only two rules to follow: use natural materials, such as pine needles, shredded bark, or wood chips, and don't cut a straight wide gash (leave that for the bulldozers), but try for gentle, meandering curves.

Thus far, we've been talking about the woodland garden you create. For those of you lucky enough to own a piece of natural woodlands or even a heavily treed suburban plot, the procedure is quite different.

Your first job is to learn what you already have and what you want to keep before you bring in new material. Here are some good basic rules:

1. If you can possibly do so, live with what you have for at least one growing season. The knowledge you gain may prevent mistakes you will later regret. Try to visualize the final effect you want to achieve; where you want clearings and where you want privacy, but don't do any cutting yet. (For the past few summers, because it is on a dirt road I frequently travel, I have watched the progress of what started out to be a cabin in the woods. Although it was close to the road, it was beautifully hidden by thick, shrubby underbrush and trees. The year after the house was completed, the immediate area around it was cleared and a lawn put in; not my taste, but not my house either. But the next summer—and this is the point of this story—the hidden house had become literally a house by the side of the road. Although all of the tall trees remained, every bit of scrubby, shrubby underbrush was neatly cleared out. The result was not only increased visibility, including car lights shining in the windows at night, but the dust of the road blew in a film over the grass, alternating in wet weather with muddy splashes. By the end of summer, something new was added: a six-foot French picket fence to do what nature had done so effectively before.

2. While premature clearing is a mistake, there are certain undesirable plants that you should remove just as soon as you recognize them. Heading the list is poison ivy or poison oak. (See the chapter on poisonous plants for techniques of removal.) If you have catbriar, greenbriar, or other brambles in the part of your woods that you want to be accessible—not on the outer perimeter—remove them too. The best way to get rid of this kind of unwanted brush is to cut the vines or stumps to the ground. If new shoots come up, as they may once or twice, cut them down again; they'll be weaker each time and eventually die. This is the easiest method and also the best, because it doesn't disturb other plant growth, and the roots of the unwanted brush remain in the earth to rot away and enrich the soil.

Depending on the size of your woodland area, how much of it you intend to develop right away, the amount of unwanted brush you have, and other factors that cannot be considered except on an individual basis, you may leave the cut brush where it is, cart it away, or throw it deeper into the woods where you cannot see it. (Be *sure* to read about poison ivy!)

3. If your property is extensive, resolve to develop only one area at a time, working from the edge nearest your house.

4. Use your first year's waiting time to learn the names of your trees; these will be your guide to the flowers you will later plant.

If you have mainly oaks and pines and other evergreens, your soil is going to be quite acid. Beech, birch, and maple indicate soil on the slightly-acid-to-neutral side. If your growth is mixed, note that too, and plant the acid-loving plants under the oaks, the neutral or slightly acid ones under the beeches. Remember that you needn't be too rigid; except in a few cases, even woodland plants tolerate a range of acidity in the soil.

Observe what your trees look like in all seasons. Unless you are good at tree identification, you had better label them. Wooden markers put into the ground make very satisfactory temporary labels. Just be sure to use indelible ink.

5. Since a certain amount of light and air are necessary even for woodland plants, you may have to do some thinning and pruning of trees before you bring in new plants.

Save your most beautiful trees. Remove small, spindly trees around them if they are preventing a good tree from developing to its most desirable form. However, don't *automatically* remove seedling trees. You want trees of all ages. Also, if you clear out too much young growth and the remaining large tree happens to die, you may have lost a good piece of your woods.

Underplant the very tall trees with lower-growing, deciduous varieties, especially the flowering ones like the dogwood. These will add great beauty to your finished garden, as well as letting in the sun in spring while providing for shade in summer. If you have specimen trees already, but they are struggling beneath dense evergreens, prune up the evergreens. Remember not to clear out all the underbrush and dead branches; leave some on the trees and some on the ground to provide nesting space and protection for birds.

6. In spring, since that is the blooming season for most woodland flowers, identify the flowers you already have. Use markers because some of the flowers lose their leaves and go dormant in summer; if you don't, you may not be able to locate them when fall comes and you are ready to plant. The usual rule, if you remember, is that you plant spring-blooming flowers in fall, and summer and fall flowers in spring.

7. If you don't already have a path, summer is the time to lay one

out. By then, everything, including the ferns, will be out of the earth. Don't be afraid to move ferns in summer; if you do it quickly and water well, they should survive. Anyway, you are better off moving them than trampling on them if they are where you want the path.

8. By the first fall, if you have had a chance to go through the spring and summer watching the growth of your woods, you should be ready to start planting, dividing, and moving wild flowers. Now you are ready to dig a bed, only of course you can't dig a bed because you are working in ground that is already a bed for all manner of growing things you don't want to disturb. Instead, you are going to have to make selective planting holes, as large as practicable, where you want to place your plants. Even so, as you know if you've done any gardening before, you are going to encounter tree roots. If they are small, simply chop into them or snip them with a pair of hand pruning shears; medium-sized ones may be cut with lopping shears or sawed off; if they are too thick for any of these methods, you'll have to move to one side or the other.

Let's suppose you've decided to put a dozen bloodroots near the edge of your woods (remember that a mass planting is almost always more effective than isolated plants in a dozen different places). Do you make a dozen individual holes? Not unless you absolutely have to. Instead, try to dig one planting hole broad enough to take all the plants; or two or three holes close together, each large enough for a number of plants. By doing this, you give the new plants room to grow and spread without immediately running into competition from existing tree roots and other plants. If you are forced to make separate holes for each plant, as you may be for certain specimens, particularly large ferns, make the hole as big as you can and be very generous with the peat moss or compost.

Water your new plants well and mulch them. If they aren't clearly visible at the time you set them out, be sure to set in markers. Woodland flowers, especially, don't like being walked over, even in winter when the ground is frozen and covered with snow.

THE WOODLAND WILDFLOWERS

In addition to the flowers listed below, be sure to look at the chapters on ferns, ground covers, and flowers for shady areas in chapter two. Look in chapter seven for suggestions if you have a brook running through your woods.

If no pH or acid-soil requirement is given for the plants on this list, you may assume they will do well in soil ranging from slightly acid (pH 6) to neutral (pH 7) or that they aren't fussy about the acid value of the soil.

Virtually all woodland flowers bloom in the spring. Since the exact date depends on the area where you live, it won't be noted here, except perhaps in general terms.

BLOODROOT
Sanguinaria canadensis

Bloodroot is likely to be among the first on anyone's list of favorite woodland wildflowers and well deserves that place. It is one of the earliest to flower, easy to grow, and fascinating to watch in all stages of its development. First to poke through the ground is its pointed closed bud, followed by a tightly furled leaf. The bud, well above the protective leaf, opens to a bright white flower, which closes again at night. It is particularly effective because nothing else seems to be alive yet in the woods. Later, as the blossom fades, the single, deeply

Bloodroot heralds the coming of spring. *(Arnold Arboretum)*

Sanguinaria canadensis

lobed round leaf begins to unfurl. It will remain decorative until late in the summer, when it disappears.

Although the bloodroot is easy to grow in almost any rich soil, I have included it here because it is so typically a woodland plant. If you don't have a woodland garden though, there is no reason why you shouldn't use it in a ground-cover planting just as you would spring bulbs.

TRILLIUM (Wake Robin)
Trillium

There is something so beautiful about the words trillium and wake robin that it comes as a bit of a rude shock to learn that a common name for the purple trillium is stinking Benjamin!

Trillium is easy to identify—three petals, three leaves—and all varieties but one are quite easy to grow. One or more varieties are native over most of the United States and also do well away from their home territory. Since they bloom at different times from very early to late spring, this makes them an interesting plant for collections. However, if you are not a trillium collector, be especially careful to include the Latin names when you order, since some of the varieties are more desirable than others. Trillium should be planted in the fall; some nurseries, in fact, will ship them only for fall planting. Cover the tuberlike rhizomes with about two inches of soil. (If rhizome-eating rodents are a problem where you live, you may want to skip this plant.)

Warning: Since you can't pick trillium without picking the leaves, don't pick it at all. Those leaves provide the food for next year's flower.

Snow Trillium (Great White Trillium)   *T. grandiflorum*

One of the great American wildflowers. The biggest, the best, the easiest of all the trillium, a must for the woodland garden. Its large white flowers are long-lasting and fade to a pinkish shade. It will grow in rich woodland soil that ranges from neutral to very acid. *T. ovatum* is the Pacific coast variety of this species.

Dwarf White Trillium   *T. nivale*

Very early, small, and charming. Use it at the edge of your woods, or along the path, where it can be seen. Good for a shaded rock garden. A western relative is *T. rivale.*

Painted Trillium   *T. undulantum*

Difficult and temperamental. Don't buy it unlessyou have very acid, cool, wet (even swampy) soil. It has wavy white petals marked at the base with red.

Nodding Trillium   *T. cernuum*

Needs moderately acid soil and moisture. Since the white flowers curve downward and tend to be hidden by their leaves, this is more interesting to collectors than to average wildflower gardeners.

Toad Trillium (Toad-shade)   *T. sessile*

Mottled leaves rest right on the ground with the red or yellow flowers held upright just above them. An interesting, ground-hugging plant, easy to grow, but frankly more a curiosity than a beauty.

Purple Trillium (Stinking Benjamin) *T. erectum*

This is a big, vigorous grower for large areas. The flowers range in color from brownish-red to maroon to red to purple and even, occasionally, to pink. Some people say there is *no* noticeable odor.

TROUT LILY (Dog's-tooth Violet, Fawn Lily)
Erythronium

A very attractive, early-blooming small flower, distinguished by its two rather large, usually mottled leaves and its nodding lilylike flower with recurved petals. Most writers complain that the Common Trout Lily, *E. americanum*, which has yellow blossoms, is rather sparing with its flowers. I don't find this to be so, but then my standards for flower performance may not be as demanding as theirs. Most of the western or midwestern trout lilies are considered to be bigger and generally superior to the eastern common trout lily. Of these, the one most frequently offered by dealers is White Trout Lily, *E. albidum*.

Erythronium americanum

A close-up of the trout lily. *(Arnold Arboretum)*

Trout lilies are hard to dig up because their little corms (shaped like a dog's tooth) tend to bury themselves deep into the ground. You are better advised to buy them.

TRAILING ARBUTUS
Epigaea repens

A flat, evergreen, ground-covering woodland plant that blooms in Massachusetts (where it is protected by a special state law) almost before the snows leave the ground. Its pink and white blossoms are extremely fragrant.

Never dig up arbutus, unless it is in the path of the bulldozer, and don't even buy it unless you can supply the extremely acid, sandy, thin soil and partial sunlight it needs to survive.

JACK-IN-THE-PULPIT
Arisaema atrorubens

One to three feet tall, stately, distinctive, and fun to look at. Even one Jack can be an asset in your garden. These are easy plants to collect (dig deep) or buy, and will thrive in almost any woodland garden if they have enough moisture.

A smaller species of Jack-in-the-pulpit is *A. triphyllum*.

Arisaema atrorubens

OCONEE BELLS
Shortia galacifolia

More often referred to by its botanical name than its common one, shortia is an excellent example of how the cultivation and sale of wild flowers can increase their number rather than endanger them.

Shortia was discovered in the late eighteenth century in the North Carolina mountains by the French collector Michaux, and then not reported again for a hundred years, during which time it became known as the "lost" wildflower of North Carolina. Shortia is native to only a few isolated spots in the Carolina mountains; however, it turned out to be very easy to propagate and perfectly hardy in even sub-zero weather; it is now one of the stand-bys of wildflower dealers everywhere.

Shortia is also one of the prettiest native woodland flowers, with white-to-pink, fringed bell-like flowers, almost an inch across, that bloom in May in the Northeast and last a considerable time. The blossoms, one to a stem, rise above a basal rosette of very bright green, shiny, evergreen leaves. Shortia is an elegant, if slow-growing, ground cover, but to my mind is more beautiful when used as an individual plant. It is particularly effective against a rock or a log.

Shortia needs moderately acid soil, shade, and moisture. Once established, the clumps can be divided after flowering.

FALSE SOLOMON'S-SEAL (False Spikenard)
Smilacina racemosa

A very popular wildflower and a good one for colonizing in large areas or toward the back of a smaller garden. The two-to-three-foot arching stems end in a feathery white plume in spring, but I think the plant is far more attractive in fall, when the berries turn red.

This plant is easy to collect and is carried by all dealers. Unlike many of the spring flowers, clumps are best divided in the spring.

HEPATICA (Liverleaf)
Hepatica

The furry little blossoms of this delightful plant range in color from white to pink or blue to lavender. It is one of the earliest flowers to bloom. (I wonder why the very earliest wildflowers are so often the most charming—perhaps to repay us for braving wet and raw spring weather to look for them.) Tuck hepatica next to a rock or a tree trunk

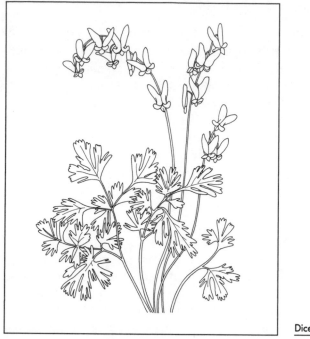

Dicentra cucullaria

or on a slope; while it needs moisture, it also needs good drainage and some sun.

If your soil is moderately acid, choose Round-Lobed Hepatica, *H. americana*. For neutral to slightly acid soil, a better choice is Sharp-Lobed Hepatica, *H. acutiloba*.

DICENTRA
Dicentra

This relative of the garden bleeding heart comes in three popular species and while they look pretty much alike, there are important differences, so read on carefully before you order any plants.

Wild Fringed Bleeding Heart *D. eximia*

By far the most adaptable of the three. It blooms in spring and then on and off all summer, and maintains its pretty foliage throughout the season. The flower is pink. It seems to do best in moderately acid soil, but will tolerate various degrees of acidity, as well as moisture.

Dutchman's Breeches   *D. cucullaria*

Has white flowers, blooms early, and then disappears. Mark its place if there is any danger of digging it up accidentally. Dutchman's breeches likes neutral soil. This is probably why it doesn't seem to do very well in the woodland wild garden, which is generally acid to some degree.

Squirrel Corn   *D. canadensis*

Similar to Dutchman's breeches, but with fragrant greenish-white flowers. It also wants neutral soil. The name squirrel corn refers to the tiny kernel-like corms from which it grows.

VIOLETS
Viola

Before I began gardening with wildflowers, I thought a violet was a violet was a violet. Now I know that the bird-foot violet and the dog violet are violets, but that the dog's-*foot* violet is a trout lily. Now I know that there are more than a hundred species of violets in the United States, and that the stemless violets have longer stems than the stemmed violets. And now that I know all that, I am tempted to say that violets are those pretty purple-blue wildflowers that everybody knows—except that some of them are white and some of them are yellow.

Fortunately, since this is not a wildflower guide book, I don't have to sort all this out and you don't have to memorize it. However, since anyone with a woodland wildflower garden is certain to want violets, and since every wildflower catalog lists as many as a dozen varieties, you really should know something about the habits (some of them pretty disreputable) of the violets you buy. In fact, I advise you to mark this page for future reference, and when you get around to ordering, check your selections against this list.

But first, the difference between the stemmed and the stemless violets: In the stemless varieties, the leaves and the flower stems grow directly from the root, in a clump. These are the lower-growing species you would choose for a ground cover or a small bed, or the front of a woodland garden (with certain reservations, to be noted later). In the stemmed violet, first the leaf stem grows up from the foot, and then the flower stem grows from the leaf axil—which is why the flowers of the stemless violets have longer stems than those of the stemmed violets. Clear?

These are the varieties most often for sale at wildflower nurseries. Although included in this list of woodland flowers, other uses are given when appropriate.

Stemless Violets

Common Violet   *Viola papilionacea*

The violet you think of when you think of violets. Deep purple-blue flower on long stems make it a good cutting flower. The large, heart-shaped leaves that grow in heavy clumps make it a desirable ground cover in the right place. It is a ferocious reproducer and its ability to throw its seeds a good fifteen feet makes it too weedy for a flower bed or a bed near a lawn. If you have a dark shady area, slightly on the dry side, it won't do too well (which is good), and it does combine beautifully with ferns and lily-of-the-valley. It is one of the few flowers that will actually thrive under a shallow-rooted Norway maple tree.

Marsh Violet   *V. cucullata*

Similar to the above, but likes moisture. In sun and shade, with the same precautions.

Sweet White Violet   *V. blanda*

A much smaller plant, and although it self-sows freely, it isn't really a pest. The short-stemmed white flowers have delicate purple veins. They do smell sweet, but you have to get pretty close. Like most violets, they do well in ordinary garden soil, and are absolutely charming combined with the tiny creeping partridgeberry or in a mossy crevice in a shady rock garden.

Bird-foot Violet   *V. pedata*

One of the few violets that is difficult to grow, but one of the prettiest, with a face that looks like a pansy. Unlike most of its relatives, this one needs full sun and sandy, acid soil. The name "bird-foot" refers to its deeply cut leaves.

Round-Leaved Yellow Violet *V. rotundifolia*

A tiny plant, native to the northern woods. It likes deep shade and wet, acid soil.

Woolly Blue Violet *V. sonaria*

Three inches or less in height, with deep purple flowers. It will grow in sun or light shade, even in poor, sandy soil.

Sand Violet *V. adunca*

Native to most of the United States in sun or light shade, and lean or sandy soil. A pretty little specimen with small blue-to-violet flowers.

STEMMED VIOLETS

Canada Violet *V. canadensis*

The plant, about twelve inches tall but somewhat sprawling, is a pretty variety for the woodland garden. The flowers are white, sometimes tinged with purple, with yellow centers. Not very showy.

Smooth Yellow Violet *V. eriocarpa*

About ten inches tall, with bright yellow flowers. Shade, moist, woodsy soil.

Dog Violet *V. conspersa*

About six inches tall with lots of pale blue blossoms held high above the leaves. Moisture, shade, and woodsy soil.

One final reminder before you go out to plant. Weeds are rarely a problem in a woodland garden. However, when you start your garden you can expect to find weeds growing along with your new plants. Pull them out by hand if you like, but never, never, never cultivate the ground. A good thick mulch around the new plants will discourage the weeds, and the summer shade will continue the job.

For further reading:

Gardening with Native Plants, Brooklyn Botanic Garden, 1000 Washington Ave., Brooklyn, N.Y. 11225 (a good source of information on wildflowers that grow in various parts of this country)

Handbook of Wild Flower Cultivation, Kathryn S. Taylor and Stephen F. Hamblin, Macmillan, N.Y., 1963

The Concise Encyclopedia of Favorite Wild Flowers, Marjorie J. Dietz, Doubleday, Garden City, N.Y., 1965

CHAPTER 6

The Seashore Garden

You can duplicate a woodland, a bog, a pond, or a meadow, but only God can make a seashore. This chapter, therefore, is directed to readers who live or vacation by the sea.

On the other hand, although you can create a formal cultivated garden in a seashore environment (and who is to say you shouldn't), this chapter is not for you either. No matter what the Sunday paper garden pages say about low-maintenance plantings for vacation gardeners, traditional gardening by the shore involves considerable attention to windbreaks, soil improvement, watering, weeding, and winter protection. Daniel J. Foley's *Gardening By the Sea* is an excellent reference for this kind of gardening.

If you love the seashore and like to garden, but don't want to be a slave to it, there is quite another way to approach the task. As with most wildflower gardens, it may involve considerable initial effort;

ABOVE: Seaside goldenrod growing in pure beach sand. *(George Taloumis)*

once established, it will be truly self-maintaining, since you cooperate with nature rather than attempt to overcome it.

Moreover, if you love the seashore and *don't* like to garden, there still may be pragmatic reasons for planting your property. In many of our most popular coastal areas, people with homes on the beaches know that a hurricane tide can sweep away a house built on or too near the protective dunes and that natural or manmade erosion can eventually topple a house off a cliff. While a single homeowner can hardly hold back an encroaching sea or support a seriously threatened cliff, more and more people have become aware, usually following a disaster, of the importance, first, of *not* building on or in front of a protective dune and, secondly, of building dunes and stabilizing the ones they already have. (Where the scope of the problem of shifting sands and disappearing dunes *is* manageable, the homeowner's first defense is American beach grass or other similar grasses. For information on the best techniques for establishing dunes in a particular site, write the Soil Conservation Service of the U.S. Department of Agriculture, Washington, D.C.)

Although less potentially disastrous than building too near the sea or the edge of a cliff, the homeowner's desire for his money's worth of view can lead to landscaping mistakes that may also be destructive in the long run. In his *Guide to Landscaping and Gardening Handbook*, Ervin G. Conley, a nurseryman of Boothbay Harbor, Maine, suggests some of the mistakes of removing important trees and shrubs:

> The folly of stripping an entire area of trees for a better view . . . comes to light when one realizes that much privacy is lost, that one has become exposed to strong winds, full sun, excessive cold, washouts, and the eventual need for replanting or screening. We also note with consternation the cutting down of all deciduous or hardwood trees, leaving only coniferous or evergreen trees such as spruce and pine with the thought, perhaps, that they are more important and more "Maine." Without the protection of the hardwood trees many of the evergreens are felled by the first strong winds and those remaining are weakened and killed by exposure to sun, wind, and cold.

THE ROCKY COASTS

Wind and salt spray are the two universal factors that govern planting at the seashore. Sand, which would seem to be the most obvious element, may not even be present. Along the rocky coasts of Maine and the Maritime Provinces of Canada, and the Pacific Northwest, much of the coastal land has soil no different from that which exists inland—under the deep spruce forests that border the very water's edge in Maine, for instance, you'll find such typical woodland species as bunchberries and ferns rather than beach grass and beach wormwood. In these areas of the seashore, the best way to discover what you can plant on your property is to observe that already grows there, for, as will be discussed below, most seashore "neighborhoods" encompass a wide variety of plant environments. For other suggestions, but mainly for sheer enjoyment of the photographs, I also recommend Eliot Porter's Sierra Club book, *Summer Island*. An abridged, paperback edition is available.

On the rocky coasts, suitable plants are easier to find than are suitable planting sites. Great sweeps of flat ledge rock or steep cliffs offer little in the way of soil to contain roots, and harsh winds are particularly unkind to tall-growing shrubs and trees, especially collected or nursery stock that doesn't have the anchorage provided by a deep root system. In nature, and this is true for both sand and rock plants, a specimen that appears from its top growth to be very young will be discovered to have developed a disproportionately deep root growth. If you've ever tried to transplant a seedling oak from a sandy dune, you know what I mean; the bottom of that root, if you can find it, indicates that your "seedling" has been around for a long, long time. I've *never* found the end of the root of a beach plum and am inclined to agree with Jean Hersey (*Wild Flowers to Know and Grow*) that there is one main beach plum root somewhere from which all others stem.

So your best bet in planting on rock is to start with very small plants, giving them extra soil if necessary, and let them develop at their own rate. Ground-hugging species that cling to and eventually spread across rocks are not only more apt to be successful, they are also more appropriate to a seashore design. Among the best shrubs for rocky sites along the shore are two creeping junipers, both native to Maine: Bar Harbor juniper and blue rug juniper, an even more prostrate variety.

Some plants that would seem ideally suited to exposed rocky conditions because of their low growth, minimal soil requirements, and ability to withstand drought and sun, are not hardy where winters are bitter and little protective snow cover is to be found; some brooms, heaths, and heathers, hardy on the West Coast, will not survive the rigors of a northern New England winter. Neither will most Alpine wildflowers. Rocky coast gardeners have enough problems to over-come without having to baby exotic or doubtful specimens.

Fortunately for the gardener, rocky coasts are not all sheer barren rock, any more than sandy coasts are all beach. For wildflowers that will grow in woods, meadows, fields, marshes, and even beaches, see the chapters approrpriate to those kinds of terrain, always bearing in mind the factors of wind and salt spray. Once again, personal obser-vation of your native flora is still your best guide.

THE SANDY SHORE

If seashore meant only the sandy strip at the very edge of the ocean, the roster of seashore plants you could grow would indeed be a slim one (and of course if your land *is* all beachfront, you will be restricted to a few varieties). But like the rocky coast, the sandy shore is a place of great variety. On Cape Cod and the islands off the Massachusetts coast, according to *Wildflowers of Cape Cod*, the following plant habitats exist:

Woodlands	Pond areas
Heathland and dunes	Boglands
Disturbed areas	Freshwater marshes and meadows
Seashore and salt marshes	Swamplands

Over 600 different plant specimens have been identified in this one seashore region. At least a third of these grow wild in other parts of the country; in fact, to belabor the point for a moment, most of the flowers listed in the seed catalog of Midwest Wild Flowers also grow on Cape Cod. George Schenk, a wildflower nurseryman of Kirkland, Washington, writes that the seeds he collected a few years ago on Cape Cod "are doing so well here I can hardly believe it after seeing how fastidiously they keep, in one case or another, to woodlands, heathlands, dunes, or disturbed areas on their native coast."

PLANTING IN SAND

When it comes to setting out new plants, the gardener at the sandy seashore undeniably faces special obstacles. If his is a vacation-home garden, he probably must do his transplanting at the least desirable time of the year, in the heat of summer. What compounds his problem, and makes it somewhat different from that of vacation-homeowners at a lake or in the mountains, is that the constant elements at his seashore are sun, wind, and burning sand, all of which have a dehydrating effect on plants. Even the foggy or rainy days, which the vacationer deplores but the gardener occasionally relishes, are of only temporary help (although they are certainly the safest days for collecting and planting).

Virtually all of the planting suggestions and tricks, some of them quite unorthodox, you will find below are designed to overcome the drying effect of the seashore environment. Naturally, you won't need to follow all of these suggestions for every plant; some won't be appropriate and some won't be necessary, especially if you can arrange to move plants in the spring or fall. And if all of what you read here seems like a lot of trouble, remember that this is a one-time investment of labor. Assuming you use appropriate plants, all you need to do is give them a fair start. Once they take hold they will thrive without further attention.

Start with small specimens. If you collect your own plants, take only small ones or the offshoot of an older plant. Although certain beach and sand plants are a cinch to dig up, some are extremely difficult, if not impossible, to move intact. Please be sure to read the directions for transplanting under the specific plants, since they vary considerably.

If you buy your plants, you are still better off with smaller rather than larger specimens. Although you may want an immediate effect, that effect is often illusory. Three years after we put in a dozen plants of *Rosa rugosa*, six large and six small, they were all about the same size. While the bigger ones were accommodating themselves to their new homes, the smaller ones were catching up. Buying small plants, therefore, not only cuts down on losses, it can stretch your plant budget considerably.

Purchasing versus collecting. All other things being equal, you are better off at the seashore with nursery-grown stock. Unfortunately, even aside from the question of expense, all other things are *not* equal, since very few nurseries carry seashore plants. They are even hard to find in the catalogs of wildflower dealers. If you do buy plants, it is even more important at the seashore than anywhere else that you get healthy potted specimens or purchase from the most reputable specialty dealers. My own experience with mail-order purchases of inexpensive so-called nursery stock has been pure disaster. Even the plants that arrived alive, and very few did, were far too weak to survive in a seashore environment.

One alternative to buying is to dig your own specimens and transplant them not into the ground but into pots of enriched soil. Then bury the pots, preferably in a spot that gets some shade, and positively in a place that is handy to your water faucet. The shade of a house is just as good as the shade of the trees you may not have. The north side of a building is the best, but the east isn't bad either, since the morning sun is never as hot as the afternoon sun.

Coffee cans make excellent starter pots for your transplants. Make half a dozen holes with a beer can opener at the bottom of the can for drainage; by the time you are ready to move the plant to its permanent location, the bottom will be partially rusted away. If you intend to leave your plant in the coffee can, as I almost always do, make some more holes with your can opener to speed the rusting process and give the roots plenty of room to come through. (One of the virtues of leaving the plants in their cans is that the roots are directed down deep into the sand or the sandy soil where they will not be hurt by the surface heat or dryness.)

Be extremely careful to bury your cans deeply enough to prevent cut feet, even of those thoughtless enough to step on your plants!

Clay or plastic flower pots are also good starter pots for your transplants, although I rather like the idea of being able to recycle the cans to get one more use out of them after the coffee is gone. Again, be sure to bury the pots in their temporary positions. If you plan to rebury them in the permanent locations, be sure to remove or make plenty of holes in the bottoms—clay or plastic will not decompose as metal will.

Very small plants may be started in the little cardboard or plastic containers that berries come in; if you use the plastic ones, line them with a layer of newspaper to keep the soil from running right out. Peat pots are also good starter-pots for small transplants. In all cases, but especially with the peat pots, be very careful not to tear up the roots that may have penetrated the pot when you move the plants to their permanent locations.

When the plants started in any of these temporary planters are ready to be moved—a time you will have to determine for yourself, based on weather, season, new growth, and your ability to supply water—you may decide to take the plant out of its pot. If so, treat it as any other transplant, and be especially careful to follow the directions for mulching.

Improving the soil. Even though seashore plants grow in pure sand or the thinnest sandy soil imaginable, it is almost always a good idea to add peat moss or other organic material (compost if you happen to have it) when you transplant. This will not only give the roots a good head start, it will retain water as sand itself will not. Oddly enough, planting right at the shoreline is somewhat easier than in the dry sandy dunes farther inland simply because the ground-water level at the beach is closer to the surface and the air is damp with spray. (Naturally, this is of no help with plants that are intolerant of salt spray, but we aren't dealing with that kind of gardening in this book.)

Fertilizing. Never use a dry chemical fertilizer on seashore plants, least of all in the heat of summer and when you are transplanting. You needn't fertilize at all when planting, but a *weak* solution of liquid fertilizer is helpful. To be extra safe, wait a few days before doing anything. Once a natural planting is established, there is no need to fertilize. However, if you want to do so, bear in mind the porosity of the sand and its surface heat. These two factors should tell you that it is both safer and more effective to apply two half-strength doses of liquid fertilizer rather than one dose at full strength.

Plant deep. Forget everything you ever learned about setting plants at their natural level and plant them deep, *several times deeper* than you ordinarily would. This is especially important in the case of trees and shrubs; indeed leggy specimens can be set in right up to their top growth. For this good advice I am grateful to William Flemer III, of Princeton Nurseries and author of an excellent book, *Nature's Guide to Successful Gardening and Landscaping*, who explains that the poor water-retention quality of sand means that the oxygen necessary for root growth can also penetrate deep into sand. By taking advantage of this knowledge, you can give your new transplants the benefit of a cool, wet root run without causing the roots and stems to rot as they would in wet soil.

(As a seashore gardener myself, I am also grateful to Mr. Flemer for explaining why the salty seashore air is something other than an obstacle to gardening. On the contrary, he suggests that the salt actually has a salutary effect on some plants because it acts as a natural fungicide. In case you have wondered why roses, lilacs, zinnias, phlox, and some other flowers that are subject to mildew and fungus in the humid inland areas in the East grow so spectacularly in coastal gardens, that is your answer. But don't take it to mean that you can plant those flowers on the beach in the face of the full ocean spray.)

Mulch. (Mulch, mulch, mulch!) Since water leaches down through the sand and evaporates up off the surface, mulching is one procedure you should never skip. Mulch at the bottom of your planting hole as well as at the top, making sure that the bottom mulch is covered with a layer of soil or sand-and-peat mix so the roots will have something to grow on. After your bottom mulch has served its first function, that of helping retain moisture, it will eventually decompose and provide food for the growing plant roots.

"Green garbage," such as the coffee grounds, lettuce leaves, and other vegetable material, are a good bottom mulch. In my own experience, unfortunately, the dogs, who wouldn't eat that stuff if I offered it to them, somehow sniff out its burial sites and like to dig it up, excavating the plant in the process. Since leaves and compost are not likely to be plentiful on your seashore property, you had perhaps better stick to peat moss or whatever other mulch you decide to use at the top of your hole.

At the suggestion of Mrs. Ann Hunt, former owner of the Tea Lane Nursery on Martha's Vineyard, I have tried crumpled up, *soaking wet* newspaper as both a bottom and a top mulch. It works very well, but you must be sure to cover the top layer with a lot of sand or it will dry up, fail to do the job, and look unsightly.

Eelgrass is a marvelous mulch for seashore gardeners. It is available, free, right where you want it; it is highly nutritious, and because it doesn't mat down can be applied very thickly. In addition, it gathers and traps moving sand, an important consideration on hillsides or dunes where erosion is a problem, or on exposed sandy places where the winds cause sand to shift. You don't have to wash the salt out of the eelgrass; watering and rain will do it for you. Actually, there is no reason to believe that the amount of salt in eelgrass will hurt the generally salt-tolerant plants of the seashore. Along the beaches of brackish ponds, you often find roses, sea lavender, goldenrod, and other plants growing up through thick layers of washed-up eelgrass. A friend who over the years had failed in her efforts to transplant beach pea claims that her first success came when she used eelgrass as a mulch. My own first success, also after a number of failures, was when I put the offshoot in a coffee can first, as described above, but since I also used eelgrass as a mulch, that experiment is not scientifically pure.

Even better than eelgrass, because it is cleaner, lighter, and therefore much easier to handle, is salt-marsh hay. As the name indicates, this is the hay from salt-marsh grasses which, very much like eelgrass, is washed up onto the shores of the marshes. You can lift it in great sheets, so take a number of large green plastic leaf bags when you go collecting and you will always have a supply on hand. Like all biodegradable organic mulches, the hay will eventually decompose to help condition the sandy soil.

With all the free mulch available near a seashore, I have never found it necessary to go out and buy any. No reason why you can't, of course. Aside from peat moss, which is universally available, your choice will be limited to what you can buy in your own locality.

Watering. Like deep planting, this is another instance where you are usually better off using a technique that is frowned upon in environments where the soil is heavy and water-retentive. The one good initial soaking, sometimes all you need to start a plant in clay, loam, or mucky earth, is not enough. The excess water quickly leaches away and, if you are planting on a hillside or a dune, will create gullies. For the same reason, an untended sprinkler can be damaging to a sandy site. After the first good soaking, the best method, I find, is the hand-held hose with the nozzle, or your thumb, positioned to guide the water into a gentle spray. Be sure to saturate the ground, but as soon as the water starts running off, stop. In hot weather, new plantings may require two waterings a day. Naturally, the more of the previous recommendations you have followed, the better your plants will be able to survive the shock of transplanting.

Planting a hill. Setting out plants on a sand dune or a bare hillside, such as that created by changing the grade around a newly built house, has its own special problems; the mere act of digging a hole for the plants is either impossible or likely to set off a small landslide.

I found my solution at the town dump, of all places, in the form of a load of old shingles stripped off a house. I imagine any pieces of short wide scrap wood would do as well, although the advantage of shingles is that they are thin at one edge and thick at another. This makes it possible to tap them deeply into the sand without setting off a small avalanche in the process. Be sure to face your wood perpendicularly *across* the face of the hill. Diagonal placing will channel the water down into gullies. For the same reason, stagger your shingles.

Leave about one-third of the shingle above ground, put eelgrass or hay *above* the shingle, and dig your hole above that. Gently! Don't dig a wide hole if you can avoid it, but do dig a deep one, since your aim is to get those roots going quickly to stabilize the loose sand. Be extremely generous with mulch. In a year or two, or whenever plant growth has taken over the job, you can pull out the shingles or break them off at ground level. Anywhere else they would decompose, but the salty seashore air tends to preserve the uncovered wood. Use them for kindling.

The best "first" plants for an interior dune, even one composed entirely of builders' fill, is beach grass—which, of course, is the obvious choice for a seaside dune. One of its great virtues is that on a very steep hill, you don't even have to make a real planting hole; just poke your sharp trowel down as far as you can and quickly tuck the root and as much of the grass blade as you can into the crevice. The deeper you go and the more you get below ground, the better off you are.

The Seashore Plants

The plants below might be described as "typical" seashore plants, those that grow on the shore dunes and the inland dunes and heathlands. However, as we have seen, "typical" seashores may, and almost always are, composed of other environments as well. For woods, meadows, roadsides, and wet places, look under the appropriate headings. An asterisk * indicates that the plant is described in another chapter.

BEACH GRASS
Ammophila

Tiny rockets, sandworts, and spurges grow even closer to water than beach grass does, but they are of little significance to the gardener. Beach grass (whose Latin name means "sand lover"), on the other hand, is invaluable. Fortunately, since you can't buy plants, it is readily available and easy to dig up and transplant. While this conflicts with what I have read elsewhere, I do *not* recommend that you dig up a large clump; it is hard work and unnecessary to dig into the middle of a stand of beach grass, and it may be destructive to the dune that grass is holding. Instead, take a plastic bag and sit on the beach (you might as well enjoy yourself) right at the point where the grass gives way to pure sand. Here is where you will find the youngest shoots of beach grass, not thick enough to be matted and not old enough to be connected to thick tough roots. With the aid of a trowel (you don't really need one—in pure sand no "soil" is going to cling to the roots anyway), gently dig in the sand around the farthest-out shoot and ease it out of the sand as far as you can. What you will end up with is a long root runner from which, at intervals, sprout individual roots and blades of grass. You can cut these up to make separate plantings of each, but it is better to clump three or four roots in one hole. If you remain to swim or sunbathe after you have finished collecting, be sure the sun doesn't bake your plastic bag; cover it with damp sand. If you are using beach grass to hold a dune or a hill, you want to give it a quick start. Fertilizing, as described above, is important in this instance. And unless you transplant in early spring or in the fall, water well.

If you like the look of a house on the dunes surrounded by nothing but great sweeps of beach grass, bear in mind two drawbacks: new shoots are exceedingly sharp and a menace to bare feet, so you must have boardwalk paths; also, large unbroken stands of beach grass can be a fire hazard, since last year's growth remains on the surface dry as straw.

BEACH WORMWOOD (Dusty Miller)
Artemisia stelleriana

Artemisia grows in large silver-gray clumps among the beach grass right on the first dune. The leaves are thicker and fleshier than the Dusty Miller we know inland, and the flowering stem, with its yellow blossoms, is the least interesting part of the plant. Wormwood is reputed to be so easy to grow that you can simply stick a piece of stem into the sand and expect it to root. I've never tried it because it is equally easy to pull up an outside shoot, not disturbing the main clump, and you *know* that will grow. It may be transplanted to a sandy inland dune, in full sun, but nowhere is it as beautiful as right on the beach.

BEACH PEA
Lathyrus japonicus

Beach pea also grows on the dunes, lying flat in curling, vinelike fashion among the beach grass. Its deep blue-violet flowers bloom all summer, and although not as showy as the everlasting pea vine or the cultivated sweet pea, they are truly beautiful and well worth trying to grow. But this is a frustrating plant—it looks so easy to transplant, in much the same way as you transplant beach grass or Artemisia, but it is actually very difficult. Your safest bet is to collect the seeds and sow them in moist sand where you want them to grow. Or try, try again, using the coffee-can method described above.

BEACH ROSE
Rosa rugosa

Everyone tells a slightly different story of how this Japanese import landed on the shores of Cape Cod about a century ago; I rather like the theory that it was among the horticultural materials on a ship that was wrecked on the beach. No matter; the Japanese sea tomato is without doubt the most desirable of all seashore shrubs. It grows wild along both coasts and is also available at some nurseries. Although its biggest display of flowers, which range from red to magenta to pink to white, is in June, the beach rose flowers all summer long, and at the same time displays its distinctive large scarlet "hips." A special glory of the beach rose is the dark green, deeply wrinkled foliage.

With thick gloves and a pair of pruning shears, cut beach roses for the house. They have a heavenly, intense "rose" smell, but don't expect to be able to do much fancy arranging; the thick thorny stems make them virtually impossible to handle.

Beach roses grow in great clumps, sometimes as much as six feet tall. If you want to keep them low and spreading, as a ground cover, prune down the tall center canes. This also makes them spread much faster.

You can collect them, or make new plantings from your own shrubs, by digging out the suckers from mature plants. Almost invariably, I have found that these new plants turn yellow and appear to die. Don't give them up for dead; they will come back. Use the beach rose right on the first dune or inland, where it makes a marvelous hedge along a rocky wall.

SEASIDE GOLDENROD
Solidago sempervirens

Seaside goldenrod grows on the shore dunes and inland, has large fleshy leaves, and big heads of bright yellow flowers are held on arching stems. In the wet atmosphere of the seashore dune, or in slightly enriched inland soil, the stems may be two or even three feet long, but along a dry dusty road you'll find specimens that look like miniatures. These last are a good source for a collector, since they couldn't be easier to dig up or transplant, and will promptly grow into great many-stemmed specimens in a wetter or richer habitat. To increase your supply, divide your established plants.

Seaside goldenrod is so showy and so easy to grow that it is unfortunate that it suffers from the same bad reputation of all goldenrods as a source of hay fever. It isn't goldenrod that causes hay fever, but ragweed, an ugly nondescript weed that sheds its pollen during the same season when goldenrod is in bloom.

GOLDEN ASTER
Chrysopsis falcata

Golden aster isn't an aster, but the yellow flowers look like their namesake. This low-growing plant does well in extremely dry, sandy soil, even right near the beach, and is found growing wild along the East Coast as far south as New Jersey.

Moving back from the seashore, the variety of plants that survive and grow naturally increases noticeably. On the other hand, these native plants are harder to transplant from the wild because of the deep, sometimes apparently endless root systems they have developed in order to reach the cool moisture well below ground level. To be successful with them, be sure to follow the planting suggestions in this chapter.

BEARBERRY *

BEACH HEATHER (False Heather, Woolly Beach Heather, Poverty Grass)
Hudsonia tomentosa

Flat, grayish-green masses of this heatherlike plant cover the dry sandy inland dunes and seem to come to life in the rain. The tiny yellow

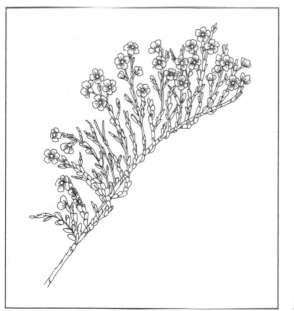

Hudsonia tomentosa

flowers appear in June. Strictly a plant for dry sandy dunes and *extremely* difficult to move. About the only way you can succeed is to keep a sharp eye out in late summer or early fall for a brand-new seedling—*not* a new offshoot of a parent plant.

A close relative, Golden Heather, *H. ericoides*, is brighter green and, possibly because it also grows on higher ground in slightly heavier soil, somewhat easier to dig up and transplant.

BEACH PLUM
Prunus maritima

An exceedingly hardy seashore shrub for sterile dry sand dunes, it grows wild along the northeast coast, although if you have read this far you have gathered that it is virtually impossible to transplant. I have never seen it listed in a nursery catalog or found it for sale. (I will be happy to stand corrected if you know of a source or have had reasonable success in transplanting the beach plum.)

As a garden specimen, seen singly, the beach plum is not the handsomest of shrubs. What *is* beautiful is to see the dry dunes covered with its clouds of pink and white flowers in late spring. But above all, the special glory of the beach plum are the plums. These grape-sized fruits, ranging in color from palest pink to deep red-purple (some varieties are golden) are inedible raw, but the source of a marvelous jelly or jam. In a good plum year, they are so profuse they almost leap into your basket. You can always tell when the fruit is ripe by the number of cars parked along the seashore road, with occupants fanned out into the bushes.

BAYBERRY
Myrica pensylvanica

Bayberry is quite another story, although it grows right along with the beach plums, in the poorest, driest sandy soil. A southern relative is the Wax Myrtle, *M. cerifera*, and the Pacific variety is *M. californica*. Another close relation is bog Myrtle, *M. Gale*.

Bayberry can be transplanted and can also be bought potted or balled-and-burlapped. I suggest that you buy plants, but if you want to collect your own, keep a sharp eye out in late summer for the small new seedlings, which are easy to dig up and replant. You can also take suckers from established plants. Keep in mind that it takes both a male and female plant to produce the distinguishing gray berries. If you already have bayberry growing wild on your land, your new

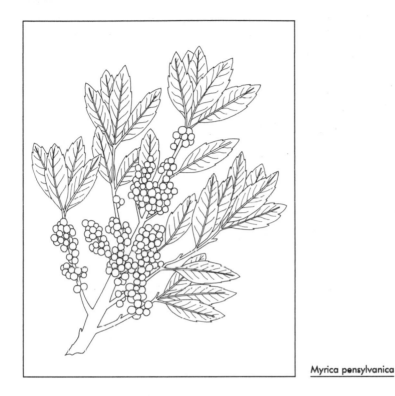

Myrica pensylvanica

plants will be fertilized by others in the area, so don't spend your money on an expensive plant unless it is clearly marked "female" or already bears berries.

SCOTCH BROOM
Cytisus scoparius

Scotch broom was brought to the Virginia shores in Colonial times, and has since naturalized itself on both the east and west coasts. It likes lots of sun and very poor dry soil. The flowers of the Scotch broom are bright yellow wands of blossoms and marvelous for flower arrangements (although I find the smell somewhat disagreeable if you get too close). A related broom is Warminster broom *C. praecox*, which is also extremely hardy but has paler yellow flowers and grows generally lower and bushier. Both of these brooms are excellent in a seashore landscape. If they begin to grow too tall and ungainly, prune them by selectively cutting back a few of the tallest branches. Don't "trim" these or any other natural shrubs as you would a privet hedge.

Brooms are virtually impossible to transplant once established—

and they established themselves very quickly. However, they are very easily purchased. In fact, in recent years they have become so deservedly popular that many different varieties, in all sizes, habits of growth, and colors are now available. Before you get carried away with the possibilities of growing a lot of different varieties yourself, check out their hardiness against your own plant-hardiness zone. Not all of the hybrids are as rugged as the ones described above, and many of the newer species are natives of southern Europe.

HIGHBUSH BLUEBERRY
Vaccinium corymbosum*

LOWBUSH BLUEBERRY
Vaccinium angustifolium*

SHADBUSH (Shadblow, Downy Shadblow, Juneberry, Serviceberry)
Amelanchier canadensis

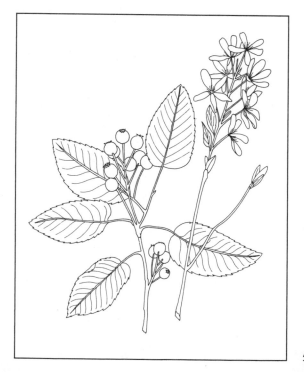

Amelanchier canadensis

A native of the northeast coast, Shadbush thrives inland as well as near the sea, and is carried by nurseries from coast to coast. Depending on where it grows, it can be a shrub or a small tree, and although it is usually found in the low wet areas between the dry dunes, I have seen beautiful specimens right *on* the dunes. Its many common names are probably a tribute to its popularity. The name "shad," by the way, comes from the fact that its white flowers bloom when the shad run in early spring.

Along the dunes and heathlands of the seashore, you'll find a wealth of collectible wildflowers (most of which can also be purchased from wildflower dealers.) So read the dos and don'ts of collecting, sharpen your eyes, take along a guide book, and look for some of these:

White Flowers

Oxeye Daisy
Queen Anne's Lace
Pearly Everlasting
Yarrow

Yellow or Orange Flowers

Evening Primrose
Buttercups
Wild Indigo
Goldenrods
Tansy
Black-eyed Susan*
Coreopsis*
Butterfly Weed*
Hawkweed

Blue or Purple Flowers

Blue-eyed Grass*
Bluets
Bird's-foot Violet*
Asters*
Purple Coneflower*
Thistle
Toadflax
Lupine*

Generally speaking, these plants are to be found on the dry dunes, heaths, meadows, and along the roads near the seashore. but even in those dry areas, there is much to remind you that water in some form is everywhere. For plants that grow in wet ground, as well as the woodland plants, look in the appropriate chapters. But most of all, look around you when you go for a walk; you are sure to find many other flowers that don't appear on any of these lists.

For further reading:
Gardening By the Sea, Daniel J. Foley, Chilton, Philadelphia, 1965

How to Hold Up a Bank, G. Reid, A.S. Barnes, Cranbury, N.J., 1970 (That's a sloping bank, not a savings bank.)

A Beachcomber's Botany, Loren C. Petry, The Chatham Conservation Foundation, Chatham, Mass., 1968 (An excellent field guide for the northeast seashore areas generally.)

Nature's Guide to Successful Gardening and Landscaping, William Flemer III, Thomas Y. Crowell, N.Y., 1972 (See particularly the chapter on seashore gardens for planting large trees and shrubs in rocky or sandy shore locations, and for good suggestions about specimens to plant. But while you are at it, do read the chapter on the garden as an ecosystem. Altogether, this is one of the best books I have read.)

CHAPTER 7

Wildflowers for Ponds, Brooks, and Soggy Soil

Moisture in a garden can be an asset or a burden. If your wet soil borders a stream, a pond, a river bank, or a natural or man-made pool, no one has to tell you that you are indeed among the luckiest of mortals; the flowers in this chapter will simply enhance an already lovely environment. More typical, unfortunately, are wet spots caused by poor drainage or low ground. As land around cities has become scarce, new houses are often built on marginal soil, bordering wetlands or actually on them—although today conservationists are beginning to convince municipalities that wetlands serve a purpose other than that of being filled in for development.

On land that is low and marshy, or where natural drainage is poor, the usual procedure is to install artificial drains and bring in additional fill to establish lawns and flower beds. This is a costly procedure and not always a permanent solution; over the years, drains clog up and if the water table is close to the surface, even filled land may eventually

---

ABOVE: Marsh marigolds brighten this soggy area where the lawn meets the road.
(M.E. Mendelson)

become water-logged. One might also question the esthetic achievement of transforming the landscape into the duplicate of every other suburban housing development. Instead of draining and filling, how much more appealing it would be to excavate part of a swampy area to create a small pond, using the material from that excavation to raise the level of the surrounding land.

As always, by working within the limitations of a natural environment, it is possible to create a garden that has both beauty and stability. Few cultivated plants can stand constantly wet feet, but many beautiful wildflowers actually demand them. Some rugged ones have such deep, tough root systems that they can be useful as well as decorative, controlling erosion along ditches, culverts, and river banks.

The plants in this chapter range from dainty, tiny flowers to massive, deep-rooted, spreading clumps. Be sure to note their habits and special requirements, if any, before making your selections. While all of them demand wet soil to grow to their fullest, some plants in this list will also grow in ordinary garden flower beds. Some of the latter will be marked with an asterisk * which means that you will find them described more fully in another chapter. None of these plants are true aquatics that must stand in water at all times of the year. This is useful to know since wet meadows, marshes, bogs, and even rivers and streams often dry up in summer.

Planting the banks and edges of watery places presents no real problem. A marsh or a bog, however, could be so completely under water in spring that you might not be able to get into it. In that case, there is nothing wrong with waiting until summer when it is drier, since the sub-surface will be moist enough for your plants (if not, you can water them in as you would anywhere else). Be careful about planting too late in fall, when the heaving of freezing and thawing ground may uproot plantings that haven't had time to get established. If you do plant in the fall, mulch deeply.

If you need to improve the humus content of your wet area, as you may if it is clay soil that has been packed down and stripped by bulldozing, wait until the earth is dry enough to be worked. Most natural wetlands are rich in humus, and you will not have to do anything to prepare them for planting.

MARSH MARIGOLD (Cowslip)
Caltha palustris

The most striking display of marsh marigolds I ever saw was along an otherwise intensely manicured street in an elegant suburb. Where every other property-owner had built up his land and planted it with grass and formal border shrubs, one had allowed the lawn to slope down naturally to the wet, marshy edge of the road. There in earliest April, under the bare branches of a giant beech tree, was a mass of shiny, yellow flowers, like huge buttercups, above bright, heart-shaped leaves. It was a stunning sight on a bleak, gray day. Later in summer, after the marsh marigold had disappeared, ferns and the low-hanging branches of the beech tree filled that area.

Marsh marigolds are so beautiful and so easy to grow that if you have any wet place at all you ought to try them. Actually, if you have plenty of moisture in spring, they can survive quite dry soil in summer. Mark their location, however, since they do lose their leaves and you might inadvertently dig them up when planting other flowers in their neighborhood.

The marsh marigold is an excellent choice in sections of the country where you have cold springs; they grow wild from Alaska to the eastern coast of Canada and as far south as Iowa in the Midwest and South Carolina in the East. Every wildflower dealer sells them, or you can grow them from seeds or division after they bloom in spring.

WILD CALLA
Calla palustris

The Latin names of marsh marigold and wild calla are deceptively similar, so be careful when you write out an order to distinguish between *Calla* and *Caltha*. *Palustris* means marsh.

Calla palustris

Wild calla is a small (five-to-ten-inch) version of the garden plant of the same name. It has waxy white flowers in late spring followed by red berries in fall. It is especially good for planting around a small pool, but it must have cool acid soil that remains moist all year.

FORGET-ME-NOT
Myosotis

The best of the forget-me-nots, and the one you are most likely to find in plant catalogs, is *M. scorpioides*, a European native plant that has escaped from gardens. It has bright blue flowers that bloom all spring and summer, and although it is a relatively short-lived perennial, it self-sows freely; once planted in a favorable spot, it will last indefinitely. This forget-me-not will thrive in sun or light shade in rich, moist soil, even in a garden bed. It is loveliest, however, at the edge of a brook or pool.

A native forget-me-not that grows in muddy soil over most of the country is *M. laxa*. The flowers are lighter blue and somewhat sparser. There are annual forget-me-nots that also self-sow, if you prefer to buy seeds.

BLUE-EYED GRASS
Sisyrinchium*

MARSH VIOLET
Viola cucullata*

SWEET WHITE VIOLET
Viola blanda*

MEADOW PHLOX
Phlox maculata

Not quite so desirable as *Phlox divaricata*, the beautiful wild blue phlox, but the best one to grow in wet meadows or a wet wild garden where the soil is fairly acid. The plant is about two feet tall, and the flowers, which bloom in late spring and early summer, range in color from white to pink to purple.

SWAMP MILKWEED
Asclepias incarnata

Another wildflower that takes second place to a gorgeous relative, in this case the butterfly weed. However, swamp milkweed can stand up for itself as a choice wildflower, and unlike the coarse purple field milkweed, it won't become a pest. The flowers are rose-purple atop three-foot stems, and they bloom in summer.

CARDINAL FLOWER
Lobelia cardinalis

A rare wildflower that you should never collect from the wild. However, since it is an all-time favorite, every dealer carries it. Cardinal flower is the brightest of all red flowers and grows in single spikes or, if you are lucky, a clump of red spikes. It will grow in average, rich garden soil, but is at its best in a wet meadow or swamp, or along a brook or stream, in sun or half-shade. It is temperamental, though; sometimes it disappears from one place to show up somewhere else. And sometimes it just disappears.

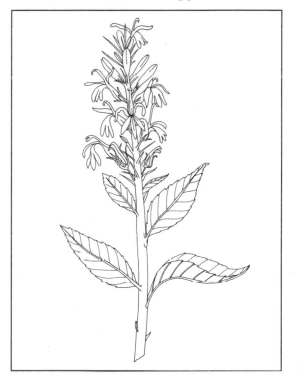

Lobelia cardinalis

Purple loosestrife, considered by some a menace because it grows so aggressively in damp swampy areas, is still a beautiful late-summer sight. Anyway, you have been warned. *(Arnold Arboretum)*

WILD IRIS
Iris

Blue Flag (Larger Blue Flag) *I. versicolor*

Virtually every part of the country has its own variety of blue flag, one of the most desirable of all wildflowers for wet soil. In spring sheets of bright purple-blue fill shallow ponds and wet swamps or meadows. *I. versicolor* is a tall, strong variety, native over most of the eastern half of the United States and Canada, and othe one most often offered by wildflower dealers.

Slender Blue Flag *I. prismatica*

Probably a better choice for smaller areas. It has narrower leaves and rather flat blue flowers. This one grows virtually down to the beaches in sandy acid soil, filling the marshes behind the dunes with the same intense blue color.

Copper Iris *I. fulva*

One of the famous native irises of Louisiana. It grows wild in ditches and streams as far north as Illinois and is hardy in the North. It is a strong plant, resembling the Siberian iris, but in a beautiful shade of reddish copper.

Yellow Flag *I. pseudacorus*

A European native, a garden escape. It is as large and as tall as the native blue flag and similar in most respects except for the color of the blossoms—sometimes it is called yellow blue flag. It will grow in standing water as well as in soil that dries out in summer.

SWAMP ROSE MALLOW
Hibiscus palustris

A very choice, tall, easily grown flower for any wet garden. It has clear bright pink flowers that bloom from late summer to early fall, a time when most wild flowers seem to be either purple or yellow. Although it is usually found along coastal ponds and marshes, it will grow almost any place, even in the average garden, if the soil is not too dry. It is easily transplanted. If you collect it, don't dig out a large

Swamp rose mallow, with its bright pink flowers, is easy to establish in low wet places. *(George Taloumis)*

mature clump, but take some of the small seedling-size plants around the edge of the clump. They dig up very easily and develop quickly. *H. moscheutos*, a more southern native, but hardy as far north as zone 5, has pink or white blossoms with red centers.

JACK-IN-THE-PULPIT
Arisaema atrorubens*

SPIDERWORT
Tradescantia virginiana*

BEE BALM (Oswego Tea)
Monarda didyma*

LILY
Lilium

The Turk's-Cap Lily   *L. superbum*

Generally considered to be the finest of all our native lilies. It is certainly the tallest and the one most prolific of blossoms—it can reach eight feet in wet, acid soil, and is said to produce anywhere from three to *forty* flowers from a single bulb. The blossoms are orange-red, speckled, with completely recurved petals. This is a true lily, not the wild tiger lily, which is a day-lily. (Incidentally, the accent is on the second syllable of *superbum*; in other words, it is superb, not a super-bum, which is the way I first read it, and still haven't been able to get it out of my head.)

Canada Lily   *L. canadense*

Grows from two to five feet tall, with drooping, spotted yellow, orange, or red flowers, on graceful long stems.

Gray's Lily   *L. grayi*

A smaller, southern version of the Canada lily, also suited for wet gardens and swampy areas.

Plant your lilies in late fall, at least five inches deep, just as you do cultivated lilies. Like cultivated lilies, these bulbs, too, are sometimes eaten by rodents.

A spectacular Turk's cap lily at the edge of a marsh near Ogunquit, Maine. *(George Taloumis)*

JOE-PYE WEED
Eupatorium purpureum

There are at least four purple species of Eupatorium that are known as Joe-Pye weed, all of them similar, but the one most often listed in dealers' catalogs is *E. purpureum*. This is a massive, tall plant, with misty purple flat-topped flowers. A stand of Joe-Pye weed is a handsome sight in late summer along wet roadsides and ditches. It is usually plentiful enough to collect, but tough to dig up; you might be better off buying it.

According to legend, Joe Pye was an Indian who used this plant to cure typhus fever.

IRONWEED
Vernonia

This is another carefree, late-summer plant for large wet areas, such as meadows or roadside ditches. The very numerous flowers, which may be bright violet-blue or pinkish purple, look like shaggy, fluffy cornflowers; they are lovely in informal flower arrangements.

Ironweed can easily be collected and self-sows readily. If you buy plants, I suggest you select Common Ironweed, also known as New York Ironweed, *V. noveboracensis*, which ranges in height from three to seven feet in the wild state. Tall Ironweed, *V. altissima*, as the name implies, grows even taller, although I rather doubt that it often reaches the ten-foot height claimed for it in some wildflower guides.

FERNS

Four large ferns that want wet soil and, like Joe-Pye weed, bee balm, spiderwort, and blue flag, are particularly good for erosion-control along ditches and culverts are:

OSTRICH FERN
Pteretis nodulosa*

CINNAMON FERN
Osmunda cinnamonea*

INTERRUPTED FERN
Osmunda claytoniana*

Joe-Pye weed grows tall and straight in wettish soil. Pick the flowers just before they open and hang them upside down to dry. They look wonderful in dried arrangements. *(Arnold Arboretum)*

ROYAL FERN
Osmunda regalis*

Although ferns are generally considered shade plants, all of these can stand sun if they are planted in very wet soil.

SHRUBS

Several of the seashore shrubs in this book are native to very wet soil:

HIGHBUSH BLUEBERRY
Vaccinium corymbosum*

SHADBUSH
Amelanchier canadensis*

BOG MYRTLE (a form of Bayberry)
Myrica gale*

A rather special, but fascinating group of plants are the "insect-eaters." At least three of them, native to wet, acid bogs and marshes, are easily procured from wildflower dealers (and should *not* be collected from the wild). If you have a natural sandy, peaty bog, or can supply enough sand and acid peat moss to make them at home around your pool—and especially if you have children—you might want to try them.

VENUS FLY-TRAP
Dionaea musciplua

A native plant of the Carolinas, the Venus fly-trap has been widely commercialized in recent years as a sort of indoor toy. I have no idea whether any of the packaged plants blooms and grows as promised, but I am instinctively suspicious. Far better to grow it in a wild garden. The fly-trap, a small plant, captures its insects on the sticky hairs that cover its leaves. As the hairs fold down to hold the captured food, the plant secretes an enzyme that digests it. Not hardy in the North.

ROUND-LEAVED SUNDEW
Drosera rotundifolia

The sundew also catches food in the hairs of its round leaves. Delicate red stems, sometimes as long as eight inches (but usually shorter) are topped with several small white flowers.

Sarracenia purpurea

PITCHER PLANTS
Sarracenia

The pitcher plants are much larger, showier, and more common than either the fly-trap or the sundew. They also have a different method of attracting and capturing their prey—they drown them in their leaves, which then digest them. (I have to confess that I am somewhat squeamish about the eating habits of this whole group of carnivorous plants.) Pitcher plants are fairly easy to grow in the proper soil, and may even be potted up in peat moss and brought into the house, if you can keep them cool.

Common Pitcher Plant   *S. purpurea*

Native from Canada to Florida, and as far west as the Rockies. Its bronze-purple leaves are mottled; its purple, pink or greenish flowers stand erect on stems a foot or more tall.

Trumpet Pitcher Plant   *S. flava*

Grows considerably taller, has large yellow flowers and light green leaves. A more southern species in the wild, it is nevertheless hardy as far north as New York City.

CHAPTER 8

How to Make
a Meadow

A meadow can be large or small, high land or low, wet or dry; the soil may be rich and loamy or sandy and infertile. Although an occasional tree or bush isn't out of place, the predominant features of a meadow are grasses and flowers, which means that whatever else it is, a meadow is sunny.

You can make a meadow out of a lawn, a pasture, a rough field, or an overgrown "waste" area, you can even carve one out of a woodland to create a feeling of open space without resorting to the formality of a lawn. Needless to say, the more meadowlike your land is to start with, the easier the work of making the meadow—and the easier it will be to maintain. While no meadow can equal the lawn in terms of maintenance, the one created from land where trees and brush were the indigenous growth cannot be neglected or eventually it will return to its natural state. Yet even this maintenance is minimal, rarely requiring more than one cutting a year.

ABOVE: Liatris, with rose-purple flowers. *(Arnold Arboretum)*

The majority of all new homes, especially those built in subdivisions for speculation, are erected on open land; obviously, it is less expensive to build where the site isn't cluttered up with trees. Like many young families moving out from the city into their first "country" home, our friends, the Ds, counted themselves lucky to find a house on two acres in a development that had once been a Long Island potato farm. It was somewhat farther from the husband's work than he would have liked, but with three children and a yearning for open space, they felt that the extra land would make up for the extra travel.

When the house was completed, the builder put in a front lawn and some fairly respectable foundation planting. What he had taken out—which they didn't discover until later—was virtually all of the rich black topsoil in which Long Island potatoes once flourished, soil that had been built up over thousands of years to cover the rocks and pebbles, or glacial "till," left in that spot at the end of the last Ice Age. It was a fascinating geology lesson, but a gardener's nightmare.

For two years our friends poured so much time and money into the creation and care of a lawn, that they had neither left over for the pleasanter aspects of gardening. Even when they had succeeded in covering the stony soil with sod, they realized that the necessary seeding, fertilizing, weed-killing, watering and mowing would go on forever. Furthermore, they were not exactly enchanted with the result; they had their longed-for open space, but the result was merely two acres of monotonous grass.

Their solution was to keep the lawn in front of the house, and just enough along the sides and back to provide a play area for the children and an outdoor sitting and entertaining area for themselves. The rest they decided to ignore for a while, to see what would happen. At that point, it wasn't a meadow that they had in mind, but rather an experiment in neglect. Since the lawn that remained was not only halved in size but located in the immediate area of the house, the time and effort spent in maintaining it was reduced by considerably *more* than half. Now, for the first time, they could devote some of their gardening energy into making flower beds.

Meanwhile, down on the unwatered, unfertilized back acre, the grass grew, but more slowly, until it reached its mature height, developed seed heads, and thinned out; no longer was it a thick, blunt-cut turf, a reminder that tomorrow at the latest, it had better be cut, but rather a field of grass—in fact, a meadow. And as the grasses grew, so did the weeds. Some of them turned out to be daisies, buttercups, wild pinks, clover, and hawkweed (or devil's paintbrush).

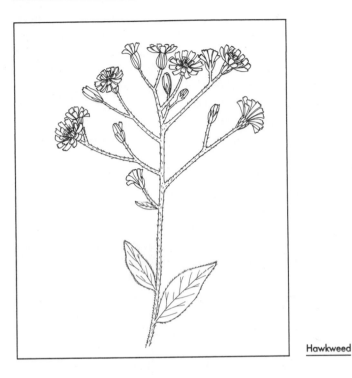

Hawkweed

Of course, it would be nice to think that every lawn weed, when allowed to develop, turned into a wildflower, but it wouldn't have been true. On the other hand, in the meadow lawn weeds were both less conspicuous and easier to pull out when full grown. Since our friends gave up pre-emergent weedkillers when they stopped tending the lawn, they expected that by the second summer the crabgrass would have become a major menace, yet oddly enough, it didn't, and the occasional full-grown crabgrass plant was also easy to pull out. Like many annoying annual weeds, the crabgrass sprouts and flourishes in sun, and the shade of taller grass creates a less favorable environment for annual weeds than does a short-cropped lawn.

Other things began to grow, too. Seedling trees, in a surprisingly short time, became young trees to be reckoned with: some should be allowed to grow, but some would have to be pulled out. After consultation with their county agricultural agent, our friends settled on a schedule of maintenance for what they now considered their meadow, rather than their experiment in neglect. Once every year or two, at the end of the summer, after the flowers had gone to seed, they would go over the meadow with a power lawn mower, to prevent the brush from getting a toe hold. Any tough or persistent scrubby vines or bushes would be pulled out at any time. And that was all.

Meanwhile, looking ahead to the need for privacy and seclusion in the growing development, they ordered inexpensive seedling trees and bushes, which they set out along the borders of the property; in that stony soil, digging a hole for a large tree or shrub was a major undertaking. For the same amount of work, they dug long trenches, filled them with good compost and peat moss, and set out a dozen or more seedlings. Moreover, since in the early years they were not "landscaping" that part of their land, they were able to place the plants well apart, allowing for later growth, without worrying about the fact that the border planting looked skimpy in the beginning. And of course, the cost was minimal compared to the cost of a major tree or specimen shrub. Also looking ahead, they planted a stand of small evergreens and oaks which would eventually provide them with a site for a woodland garden.

Although their original purpose had been to cut garden maintenance down to a manageable level, our friends, and especially their children, began to find the meadow a source of delight in itself; each year there were new surprises, new flowers (from seeds dropped by the birds, perhaps) where there had been none before. With their eyes opened to the possibility of great patches of spring or summer color, they began collecting plants and seeds to add to their meadow. In short, they had become wildflower gardeners.

Virtually any wildflower that grows in sun is suitable for a meadow, and you will find suggestions for plants throughout this book. You'll find dozens of other varieties, not listed here, by simple observation of the fields and roadsides in your own area. (You may never have noticed individual flowers there before; one of the most striking things about the hobby of wildflower gardening is the way it sharpens your eyes to what is growing around you.) Just keep in mind the predominant characteristic of your own meadow: is it sandy? dry? marshy? rich and loamy? In addition to sun, these are the factors that will determine your choice of flowers. But even these qualifications don't have to be overly restrictive, since wild meadow flowers as a whole are a hardy breed, and most of them will adapt themselves to a number of environments.

One labor-saving trick you can use in any meadow planting is to weed and plant in one step. In other words, dig out a deep-rooted weed and use that same hole to plant one of your collected flowers. You will not only save work, you will lessen the chance that the weed, or another one, will come back in the bare dirt of that spot. You can also take a single large clump of daisies, for example, collected from the wild and pull the clump gently apart into many individual daisies. Put each of these in a different spot. They grow so quickly that each of your individual plants will have grown into a sizeable clump within a year. In this way, dividing your own large clumps, you can cover a large meadow with daisies in a very few years. You will be helped along, of course, by the plant's natural ability to reseed itself.

CHAPTER 9

Poisonous Plants
and Edible Plants

Wildflowers are no more likely to be poisonous than are cultivated ones, and the only reason to include them in this book, particularly in juxtaposition with edible plants, is because collecting them for food has become a popular outdoor sport. Until recently, when everything written on the subject was the work of experienced and expert naturalists, and the devotees of eating "wild" were responsible adults, the sport was probably a lot more harmless than skiing.

What disturbs me, however, are the kind of popular books and articles that gives a cursory nod to the fact that "a few" wild plants are poisonous, as are "certain mushrooms," and then exhorts us to take the children and get out there into the wilds and taste! experiment! get back to the pioneer way of life!

Please *don't* experiment unless you truly know what you are doing. And just because you read it somewhere (including here, I have no doubt) doesn't mean it is necessarily true. For example:

ABOVE: The flowers of the highbush blueberry. *(Arnold Arboretum)*

"Though Water Hemlock (*Cicuta maculata*) is related to the Hemlock that poisoned Socrates, it is quite safe to raise . . ." says one author. But:

"Spotted Cowbane *Circuta maculata . . .beware of this plant; all parts are deadly poisonous if eaten.*" Thus reads, italics and all, the description of the identical plant in a guidebook.

Water hemlock and spotted cowbane are, as the scientific name tells us, the same plant. If the first writer were merely wrong (as indeed he is), that would not be a serious matter. However, in a different chapter in that same book, we read, "What we bring home from the wilds to eat or use is invariably satisfying and fun," and although a few poisonous plants are named, *Cicuta maculata* is not on the list.

(Parenthetically, unless you are an expert at wildflower identification, you ought to keep away from *all* members of the wild parsley family, of which the most familiar is Queen Anne's lace, or wild carrot. Some of the species are tasty and harmless, but several in addition to *Cicuta* are very poisonous, and to the untrained eye they look very similar.)

So the first thing to do is to teach a child not to put any part of any plant in his mouth without asking permission, and the second is to take an authoritative guide to edible plants *and* a good wildflower identification guide with you when you go forth to gather food from the wild.

However, there is another side to the coin—the equally irresponsible scare articles on "sinister," "deadly," or "poisonous" plants that have in recent years aroused wholly unwarranted anxiety among parents and others concerned over the safety of children. As the editor of *Horticulture* magazine points out, the word *poison* is usually interpreted to mean *deadly*, when it actually refers to any toxic reaction, from a simple skin rash or stomach upset to more serious complications. Thus, a booklet by a physician could state (accurately) that "in 1967, 2,890 poisonings by plants occurred"—yet the real truth, which he did not say, was that in 1967 the statistics of the National Clearing House for Poison Controls Centers showed 2,890 cases of "*toxic reaction* to the ingestion of plants.*"

One article that created enormous concern among parents, because it appeared in a respectable popular health magazine, contained the statement that "of the 13,000 persons stricken by plant poisoning last year, some fatally, 12,000 were children." No wonder they were worried. But aside from the use of the word "poisoning" for "toxic reactions," the editor of *Horticulture* discovered upon checking that the phrase "some fatally" actually referred to one person.

As for the "death-dealing wild cherry" mentioned in the same article, that's pretty scary unless you happen to know:

1. That the fruit of the wild cherry is so bitter as to be virtually inedible;

2. That it isn't the cherry that's "poisonous" but the young shoots and leaves and, according to some people, possibly the pits;

3. That the pits and seeds of the following edible fruits are also poisonous: peaches, plums, cultivated cherries, apricots, apples, and grapes. But you'd have to consume an enormous amount of any of these to get a toxic reaction!

As far as bringing poisonous (toxic) plants into the garden, few wildflowers can match the poisonous qualities of the cultivated monkshood (aconite), belladonna (atropine), and foxglove (digitalis). And none of us is about to rip out the yews, rhododendrons, wisteria, larkspur, lupines, delphinium, or the dozens of other garden plants that are poisonous to some degree if eaten. Still, there's no point in asking for trouble, and if a plant is known to be poisonous, and at the same time looks edible to a small child, I would consider it an attractive nuisance and avoid purposely planting it—especially if it has appealingly pretty fruits or berries.

The fast-growing bitter nightshade vine, *Solanum dulcamara*, is common throughout the United States. With its deep purple flowers and bright red oval berries, described by Thoreau as hanging "more gracefully over the river than any pendant in a lady's ear," it seemed for a while as if this vine would be a perfect cover for the raw foundation of our new house near the beach. But the more flowers and berries it produced, the more nervous we got—because of its prominent location, clearly this *was* an attractive nuisance—until finally, reluctantly, we pulled it out. Before you rush to tear out your own vines, let me point out that this bitter nightshade, although toxic, is not the black or deadly nightshade, *S. nigrum*. The latter has *white* flowers and *black* berries. The popular Jerusalem cherry house plant, *S. Pseudo-capsicum* is a member of the same family, and children should be warned against tasting those berries, too.

Another plant I would not purposely grow, although it is a popular wildflower sold by all dealers is the white baneberry, *Actaea alba*. Although both the red, *A. rubra*, and white baneberry are poisonous, it is the white variety with its "doll's-eye" berries that is uniquely appealing to children.

For the most part, though, the really poisonous plants are of no particular garden value. Neither are they likely to be eaten; either the taste is terrible or the toxic part is well hidden and not apparently edible, as are the berries of the nightshade or the doll's-eyes. With a little common sense, there is no reason to be either foolhardy or overfearful about the dangers of eating poisonous plants.

There is, however, another type of plant poisoning that is relevant to the wildflower gardener, especially the one who has country property or collects specimens from the wild. This, of course, is the contact-poisonous plant, specifically those of the *Rhus* genus: poison ivy, poison oak, and poison sumac.

Poison ivy, *Rhus radicans*, is a true native plant; ivy poisoning was described in the days of Captain John Smith and long before that in primitive Indian cultures. Although practically anyone can tell you that poison ivy has "three shiny leaves"—more accurately, they are leaflets—the single most common cause of ivy poisoning is failure to identify the plant. Most people really don't know it when they see it.

Poison Ivy

Depending on where it grows, poison ivy may be a flat, weak, trailing, or creeping vine, vigorous, ropy, tree-climbing vine, or a tall shrub with an upright trunk and spreading branches. The leaves vary in size, color, even in shape. In the sun, especially on the sand dunes, where there are no other similar plants, poison ivy leaves are shiny and easy to identify. In shade and moisture, the leaves are dark green, rather dull, and often very large. Poison ivy that grows in full sun turns a brilliant red in fall. The clusters of waxy, grayish-white berries often go unnoticed until late fall when the leaves are gone. Unfortunately, the birds love the berries and help spread this wholly undesirable plant by dropping their seeds in ever-new places. (Talk about invasive plants! Some island places, like Martha's Vineyard, could be accurately described as bodies of poison ivy surrounded by water.)

Poison ivy and its close western relative, poison oak, *Rhus diversiloba*, which resembles it closely in appearance and effect, grow throughout the United States. Although poison ivy can be found almost anywhere, it does prefer certain kinds of environment—coastal sand dunes, flood plains, bottom lands, lake shores. Poison oak extends from Canada to Baja California and is ubiquitous west of the Sierra Nevadas and the Mohave desert. An eastern variety of poison oak grows from southern New Jersey south along the coast and as far west as eastern Texas.

The poisoning from ivy and oak is identical, and the plants should be avoided, even by those who consider themselves to be immune, since modern theory holds that repeated contact increases, rather than reduces, the possibility of becoming sensitive to the plant.

If poison ivy is growing on your own property, try to get rid of it or at least control its growth to keep it back from where people may accidentally come in contact with it.

An occasional, isolated plant is easy to eradicate either by spraying with an aerosol can of poison-ivy control (a number are on the market) or by digging it up and leaving it to die. If you are truly infested with poison ivy, digging isn't feasible: you can't get at it. Neither is cutting it down and then spraying the roots, the other method usually recommended, since you won't be able to find or reach the roots without getting all tangled up in the plant yourself. What you need is a sprayer that shoots a long, thin stream and shoots it far, so you can hit the poison ivy at a distance without raining the poison down on desirable plants. A tank-type sprayer is the best and although quite expensive, well worth the investment if you have a lot of the ivy. For one thing, it is virtually impossible to get rid of it all at once. You'll have to spray the nearest areas the first year, then wait until next year when that ivy is completely dead to get further into the brush to reach another stand. Don't be overly concerned about getting some spray on the other plants; if they aren't completely soaked, they'll come back. Similarly, if you don't completely kill a poison ivy plant, you can always go back for another shot at it.

No matter how little or how much poison ivy you have, or how you choose to eradicate it, here are two "don'ts" you must observe:

1. *Never* pull it up, no matter what time of the year; it is poisonous even when not in leaf.

2. *Never* burn the plants you have dug up or cut off even if you think they are dead because you may be wrong and the droplets of sap are carried by the smoke; some of the most severe reactions have occurred when highly suceptible persons have breathed the smoke of a fire fed by "dead" poison ivy.

Although the poisonous properties of poison sumac, *Rhus vernix*, are, if anything, more vicious than those of poison ivy, the plant is considerably less of a menace since it is not nearly as ubiquitous as the former and can easily be distinguished from the harmless sumacs. The nonpoisonous sumacs have *erect* fruits or berries that turn red when they are ripe; the plant grows in dry, sandy, gravelly places. Poison sumac has a weak, hanging, cream-colored fruit; it grows in bogs, swamps, and other low, wet places. Keep away from it.

And now to the pleasanter plants. The list below doesn't pretend to cover even a majority of plants that might be considered edible. The plants here are both good to eat and good to look at. Chickweed, dandelions, and plantain may make delicious salads, but who wants them in the garden? No so-called "survival" foods—those you can eat if the alternative is starving to death—either. An asterisk * means that the plant is discussed more fully in another chapter.

WILD STRAWBERRY
Fragaria

This is a truly delicious, fast-growing ground cover in ordinary garden soil in sun or partial shade. Even if the birds beat you to them, wild strawberries can stand on their own as a decorative plant. The leaves are dark green and the flowers white, and no one has to tell you what strawberries taste like. These smaller, often pointier gems seem twice as good as the cultivated kind.

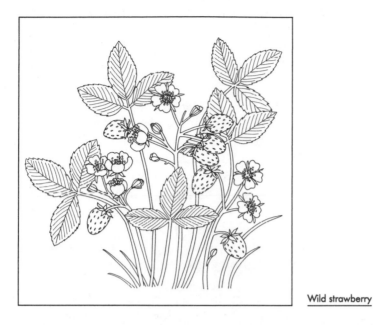

Wild strawberry

Strawberry plants are easy to move from the woods or meadows where they abound. Most dealers of wildflowers also carry them. One word of caution: let them compete with other wild grasses and flowers and keep them out of your best flower bed or they will take over. One spring I planted about ten small specimens along the border of a perennial bed and then went away for the summer. By fall I had a solid bed of strawberry vines; if there were berries, I assume the birds ate them. (Actually, I guess that wasn't so bad; the alternative would have been weeds. Furthermore, unlike some other invasive plants, the strawberry is easy to pull up.)

WILD BLACKBERRY
Rubus

Because of its vicious prickly brambles, an untended wild blackberry is ill-suited for most gardens. If you decide to grow this one, resolve to keep it in bounds by judicious pruning of the canes, and use it on rough banks, stone walls, or in a barrier planting to repel intruders. The white flower in spring is considerably larger than that of the strawberry; it somewhat resembles a single-petaled rose.

The smaller dewberry, another member of the genus *Rubus*, is a slender trailing vine, is far less prickly, and has very small berries. They taste just like blackberries, but since it takes so many to get a mouthful or a teaspoon of jam, it hardly seems worthwhile to bother to transplant these.

BLUEBERRY
Vaccinium

The Lowbush Blueberry, *V. angustifolium*, is the variety that grows in high, dry, sandy, acid soil. It is a shrubby plant, rarely more than a foot tall. The urn-shaped white-to-pink flowers are followed by berries that vary in color from light blue to purplish black.

The Highbush Blueberry, *V. corymbosum*, grows in low, wet, acid ground, usually near the seashore. The flowers, fruits, and brilliant red fall coloring are the same as those of its relative; only the height of the bush, as the name implies, is different.

So when you plant or transplant, keep in mind: low wet ground for the highbush blueberry; high dry ground for the lowbush blueberry.

The way to distinguish between the blueberry, *Vaccinium*, and the Huckleberry, *Gaylussacia*, is not by the color of the berries (since blueberries are sometimes almost black), but by the seeds. The blueberry has many soft tiny seeds. The huckleberry has ten hard seeds, which give it a slightly gritty or crunchy feel. Unlike the blueberries, which are extensively cultivated and which also hybridize among themselves, huckleberries are always wild. They do not cross with blueberries.

WILD GRAPE
Vitis

Wild grapes of one variety or another grow all over the United States. Their large leaves make them a plant for big places. Although some of them have been domesticated, don't count on the wild vines for table grapes or wine. Some of them do make a delicious jam or jelly and are fun to gather in late summer or early fall.

BEACH ROSE
Rosa rugosa*

An incredibly high Vitamin C content makes the hip (or fruit) of the beach rose a very popular health food, although it can't compare in taste with the fruits and berries we've discussed so far. On the other hand, the plant itself is far more ornamental. You can eat the hips raw or make them into a jelly. Not a native plant.

BEACH PLUM
Prunus maritima*

MINT
Mentha

The plant can be invasive in very rich garden soil, so contain it or starve it, but do try to grow some if only for the delicious fragrance of the leaves. Use them raw as a garnish for iced fruit drinks or fruit salad, or cooked for a sauce, a stuffing for lamb, or a jelly.

The three most common varieties in this country are the native wild mint, *M. arvensis*, also the introduced Peppermint, *M. piperita*, and Spearmint, *M. spicata*.

For further reading:
Stalking the Wild Asparagus, Euell Gibbons, David McKay Company, N.Y., 1962
The Edible Wild, Berndt Berglund and Clare E. Bolstry, Charles Scribner's Sons, N.Y., 1971

CHAPTER 10

Collecting—and Conserving—Wildflowers

The first thing I promised myself when I started this book was that I would not be dogmatic about the where and how of growing, planting, and collecting wildflowers, since in part it was the contradictory information I found elsewhere that provided the impetus for this project. Not only did experts contradict each other, but much of what I read was contrary to my own observations and experience. Alas, I have discovered that unless one inserts the words "probably," "generally speaking," or "on the other hand" in every sentence, it is almost impossible not to make dogmatic statements. So, with apologies, I remind the reader that (in general) the word "usually" should (probably) be used before (almost) every statement of fact; on the other hand, there are some unbreakable rules that must be followed (unless, of course, there are reasons of circumstance or the reader's own experience that decree otherwise).

All of this is particularly true when it comes to laying down rules for collecting plants from the wild to transplant to your own garden.

ABOVE: *Coreopsis verticillata* is a bright plant with neat manners for a sunny flower bed. *(George Schenk)*

Even "collecting" is a problem word. Some nature lovers will interpret it to mean robbing a woods of a rare endangered species, while what you may actually be talking about is digging up a clump of buttercups from a vacant lot.

Although lists of "protected plants" might seem to be the obvious guide to what is or is not collectible, for sheer frustration I recommend the experience of trying to make sense of a protected-plant list. Even one as authoritative as that published by the New England Wild Flower Society isn't completely useful for collectors since it lists plants that may or may not be *picked*.

I used to assume that a protected plant had to be rare, in danger of extinction, historic, or that it simply wouldn't survive transplanting. I am no longer so sure, and the more lists I see, the less sense I can make of them. As I write this, I have before me a recent book that lists "Native Plants to Protect." Along with flowers that do indeed fall into the categories above, the list includes orange hawkweed, thistle, and the black nightshade vine—all very pretty, but all common weeds everywhere, and not one of them a native plant.

If lists like this are meaningless, as I think they are, there is yet another difficulty in interpreting them, and that is in deciding what the word "protected" really means. Protected against picking or digging or both? And where? On your property or mine? Surely, no law can forbid anyone to dig up any plant, no matter how unwisely, from his own land. And just as surely, it is against all trespass laws to take any plant, protected or not, from someone else's private property without permission. When has the fact that a plant is protected, even by rare state law, ever stopped a bulldozer from ripping up millions of wildflowers in order to build a throughway?

Massachusetts, one of the few states actually to put plants under legal protection, has a law to protect its state flower, the trailing arbutus (or mayflower), and another to protect wild orchids, wild azaleas, and the cardinal flower. If you read the laws, however, you find that they refer to "pulling up or digging" or injuring the plant "except insofar as is reasonably necessary to procure the flower." Furthermore, the laws refer only to land adjoining state highways and public property, and private property without permission of the land-owner. As you can see, laws like this, even if enforced, aren't going to protect many plants; the mere act of picking a lady slipper, no matter how carefully done, will kill that plant. (The law protecting arbutus carries a fifty-dollar fine, which may be doubled if a person does "any of the aforesaid acts while in disguise or secretly in the night time . . ."—a rather charming criminal picture to conjure up.)

If legal protection isn't the answer and the published lists don't seem to make very much sense, that still doesn't relieve us of the obligation to do everything we can to preserve our heritage of wild-flowers—and not just the rare, endangered species, but those that grow by the side of the road, which should be left alone for others to enjoy. If you must collect along the roads, you might pick up a few beer cans and go off the road for your flowers. Be sure to ask permission if you are on private property.

In spite of what I have said about the value of protected-plant lists, please do get in touch with your local garden club, conservation society, or state department of conservation to find out which plants in your area are in need of protection.

The southern region of the United States Forest Service publishes a very beautiful, extremely useful, pamphlet on "Rare and Uncommon Wild Flowers" found in the national forests of Virginia, Kentucky, Arkansas, eastern Texas and Oklahoma, and all of the states in the South. The pamphlet contains a self-addressed postcard listing the plants, with the request that you help the forest service protect them by identifying the forests where you find them. In addition to publishing this booklet, the southern region protects the wildflowers in its forests by asking conservation groups and garden clubs to remove and replant flowers that are in the way of road construction within the forests. It is an example other communities might copy. For a copy of this pamphlet, write: Regional Forester, U.S. Forest Service, 1720 Peachtree Road, N.W., Atlanta, Ga. 30309.

If you live in New England, the address of the New England Wild Flower Society is: Garden in the Woods, Hemenway Road, Framingham, Mass. 01701. Excerpts from the society's list of plants to be protected appear in this chapter under wildflowers that may, or may not, be picked. If you are new to the subject of rare wildflowers, these lists are a good introduction, because plants that shouldn't be picked should never be dug up either.

After all of these caveats and "don'ts," it is time to say, on the other hand, that all rules about protected plants are off if the plants are about to be destroyed by a bulldozer. In fact, the best way for a wildflower collector to get a large supply of choice plants is by keeping a watch out for new roads or home developments. If you see any signs of new construction, check into it quickly because you must get there *before* the bulldozers. I once, like a good little citizen, passed up a remarkably beautiful stand of many different wildflowers because they were along the side of the road. Less than a week later I drove by to find that the entire roadside had disappeared, victim of what was, too late, generally agreed to be an unnecessary road-widening project. These days, citizens' groups and conservation organizations tend to be more watchful, and if you see any signs of impending activity (day-glo markers or yellow-paint hieroglyphics on the road), the local groups can probably tell you what is going on.

Some plants are easy to dig up and transplant, some are difficult, and some (bearing in mind the exception noted above) should only be acquired by purchase. For culture and planting instructions for specific flowers, look up the plant in the index and read the chapter devoted to that kind of plant.

In general, plants that bloom in spring should be moved after they have finished blooming; plants that flower in late summer or early fall should be dug up in the spring. Some people, and I am one of them, find they almost always have better luck moving plants in spring, when there is a long stretch of gardening season during which to care for them. Theoretically, you shouldn't transplant a flower when it is in bloom, but it is often perfectly practical to do so, especially since your own timetable may not permit you to be in the vicinity at the optimum transplanting time. Some plants you may not recognize until you see them in flower; others may go dormant and disappear after flowering. Use your judgment.

More important than the time of year is the time of day. If you have to decide between a cooling dip in the ocean or a collecting expedition, go for a swim; it's not a good time to collect anyway. In summer, the best collecting days are cool and cloudy, and the best times of day are morning or early evening. Although you should try to get your plants into the ground as quickly as possible, if a cool morning has given way to a hot midday when you get home, they'll be better off remaining in their bags in a shady protected place until evening. Don't let them dry out, but don't soak them either or they will rot. Always remember to keep plastic bags out of the sun. Damp newspaper, an overturned bushel basket, or wet burlap are good insulators against heat.

The collector's tools are simple, but important.

Bushel baskets and burlap are no longer as essential as they were in the days before plastic bags, but they are still useful if you have them. Newspaper (and lots of it) is good for plants and will protect your car. A jug of water or a wide-necked thermos full of ice cubes, or both, is always useful, but on a hot day, especially when the ground is dry, it is essential.

A narrow "lady spade" makes sharper, cleaner holes with less destruction to the surrounding vegetation than does the ordinary rounded, wide garden spade. It is also much easier to use. Similarly, a sharp, pointed bulb trowel is much easier to use than the wide garden trowel.

A hand pruning shears is a must, since most wildflowers are entangled in the roots of trees or other plants. Cut these away, don't pull them. Also, although you want to get the whole root system of your specimen, you can't always do so, and this means you'll have to cut it loose.

Don't forget a pencil and a pad of small-sized paper. You can't rely on your memory, so write down the name of the plant, the conditions under which you found it, including the names of the surrounding trees and plants, and put the paper in the bag that contains the plant. If you use a pen, be sure it's indelible, or you'll arrive home with nothing but a blur.

In all cases, except in pure sand where it isn't possible, take the plant with a goodly amount of its own soil attached to the roots. If possible, keep the roots totally encased in their ball of earth. (This isn't always possible.) Once again, use your judgment; this isn't so important with "weedy" roadside types like daisies and black-eyed Susans, but it is absolutely essential with flowers that grow in highly specialized environments, like the woods or bogs.

Some plants that creep along the surface of the soil, putting down roots wherever they touch, seem to ask to be pulled up by hand. Don't do it. Always take ground covers in sods, and make the sods at least ten inches square. If the plant is bearberry, don't even try taking it in sods; it won't transplant, unless the ground is frozen and you are an expert wildflower grower.

If you decide to dig up a plant and then find it is too hard to get, please restore the earth and use a little of your water to save the plant. In any case, after you have taken your own plant, do tidy up the area and replant any small seedlings that may be disturbed.

Don't ever denude an area of any kind of plant.

Many of the easy wildflowers, like daisies, common violets, some ferns, and other roadside varieties in particular, can be divided when you get home, so you can afford not to be greedy (which you shouldn't be anyway). One large clump dug from the wild can provide you with a great many little plants when you get home. This is a good labor-saving point to remember, since it involves less heavy digging and much easier transplanting. However, if you are dealing with very fragile flowers, even those that can be divided should be replanted intact. Later, when they have recovered from the shock of transplanting, you can divide them up.

As soon as you dig up a plant, put it into its plastic bag (or piece of burlap) and tie it up. Generally speaking, it is better to tie the bag around the root ball, if you were able to get a good one, than over the entire plant, since too much dampness and confinement may cause the top to wilt. But again, this is a variable matter. Sometimes one way is better than the other, depending on the size of the plant, the length of time you will be out, and your own experience. After a bit, you'll find out which seems to work best under what conditions. After all of your plants are in the car (which I hope you parked in the shade!) you can cover them all with dampened newspaper or burlap.

No matter how many plants are available for the taking, do keep in mind that they will all have to be replanted when you get home. It is far better to go back another day than to bring home more specimens than you can get into the ground with reasonable speed. Of course, if you are a step ahead of the bulldozers, this is another of those rules to be broken. Take everything you can, and then share it with others or protect it as best you can until you can replant it.

With all the care you take, a plant dug up from the wild is going to suffer more shock in transplanting than a nursery-grown specimen whose roots, having been potted or root-pruned, will not be disturbed. Therefore, in addition to following the usual transplanting techniques, you must expect to give your collected plants some extra babying— extra mulch, plenty of water, and extra shade where necessary, even for sun-loving specimens. Particularly for these, I guess, since you won't be putting shade plants in the sun anyway. At least I hope you won't. An easy way to provide temporary shade is to cut leafy tree branches and stick them in the ground around your new plantings. Or lay the branches *lightly* over them.

If your collected plants are trees or shrubs or ferns or any plants with a lot of top growth, pruning them back, often drastically, after planting will help to compensate for the inevitable destruction of some of the roots. If you are a new gardener, it may hurt you to do this, especially if you have succeeded in transplanting a good-sized tree or shrub. I can only say that the bigger it is, the more important it is to prune it severely. It's often the difference between life and death.

COLLECTING SEEDS

One possible way of collecting the wildflowers that you cannot, for one reason or another, dig up is by collecting their seeds. This is not, I must tell you, as easy as it sounds, nor is it a very effective way to collect choice plants. To take an extreme example, the great snow trillium may take from five to ten years to reach flowering size when grown from seed.

Advice on seed collecting usually begins: Collect ripe seed. There's the first rub; when you stop to think about it, exactly how do you know when the seed is ripe? Well, when it falls to the ground or flies away, or course, but that is too late. Do you have to be there at the exact moment before it leaves the mother plant, or can you take it earlier? If so, is it "ripe" or will it ripen off the plant? Sometimes one is advised to tie a bag over the seed head and come back when the seed has fallen into the bag. In general, one reads, seeds ripen within a month after flowering, but that still does not answer the questions I have just raised.

(I don't want to sound too stupid. Sometimes it is perfectly obvious when seeds are ripe, and some plants are easily raised from collected seed. What I am discussing here is seed collection in general as an alternative to collecting plants.)

Mr. L. H. Busker, an electrical engineer of Rockton, Ill., whose hobby is raising plants from seed, some years ago began to collect and study the seeds of wildflowers. In 1969, he published his first catalog of "Midwest Wildflowers" and began offering collected seeds for sale. From his experience, he says, "collecting is an arduous business. . . . Mosquitos, poison ivy, nettles, and the heat and moisture of the woods are all hazards of the trade, and I am not sure in which order they rank." As for when seeds are ripe, "There is no foolproof way of telling, but a little bit of common sense combined with a large dose of observation and an equal portion of good record-keeping will usually lead to the proper time of harvest."

Collecting the seeds isn't the end of the story. Now you want to get them to grow. Unlike the seeds you buy, the ones you collect haven't been conditioned to germinate, and they don't come with planting instructions. The serious seed collector, therefore, will have to know a lot more about propagation than can be learned in a book like this. You'll need to know about germination times, temperatures, and other techniques. Some seeds, like that of the everlasting pea vine, seem to sprout virtually upon touching the ground, but some take two years or even more; some should be planted in fall, some in spring; some need to be stratified, some soaked, some refrigerated; some can be started in one place and moved, some cannot.

If you plan to collect seeds, you should read up on seed propagation in general and then be prepared to experiment, since very little specific information is available on the individual requirements of wildflowers. Mr. Busker has been conducting germination studies on about seventy-five different species, and when his material is published, the story should be quite different. (This information is available for California gardeners from the Santa Barbara Botanic Gardens, which publishes a leaflet on the collection and propagation of native California plants—more than 350 of them! Since wildflowers do cross state lines, this information should also be useful to seed collectors in other western states.)

After all of this negativism, the fact remains that you really have nothing to lose by simply sowing seed on compatible, hospitable soil and then waiting to see what happens. By compatible and hospitable, I mean soil that is suited to the culture of the plant and not already overgrown with competing vegetation. One choice wildflower that is easily propagated in this way is the beach rose; many people have great success in spreading their plants simply by throwing the hips around in the open sand—their natural environment and one *not* already covered with other growth. On the other hand, the beach pea grows in this same environment, and even though it is related to the easily propagated everlasting pea, it won't grow for you in this manner. So there you are.

PLEASE *Do* PICK THE DAISIES

It isn't "wrong" to pick wildflowers. It's just wrong to pick the wrong ones or to pick any of them the wrong way. I have noticed that children who wouldn't dare yank up flowers in mother's garden don't have any of that respect when it comes to wildflowers, obviously because they haven't been taught. But children aren't the only ones. A surprising number of adults seem to assume that just because a flower is wild, it is tough. Actually the contrary is more likely to be true, as anyone who has picked a bunch of blossoms in the country, only to arrive home with a wilted mess of dead flowers, has discovered.

The fact is, of course, that you wouldn't pick a bunch of peonies on a hot day, put them in the car, and expect them to be alive hours later when you got home. Neither would you pick peonies by yanking or tugging at their stems. A few flowers do have brittle stems and can be picked by hand, but most don't. If you go for a walk or a ride in the country, be prepared with a hand pruning shears, a few plastic bags, and if possible some water or ice cubes. If you can't get the flowers into water, at least put ice cubes or a few drops from the thermos in the plastic bags, or wrap the stems in a wet paper napkin before enclosing them in the bags.

The lists below of Pick and Don't Pick flowers is an abbreviated version of those published by the New England Wild Flower Society. I have purposely omitted a long intermediary list of flowers that may be picked "in moderation where abundant," because this is too variable a factor to consider in a book like this. Although these lists are a good *general* guide to the northern part of the country as far west as the Mississippi River, I would urge you again to get in touch with your local garden club, conservation society, or state department of conservation for a list of plants in your own area that should be protected from picking or digging.

And please remember, *if you can't identify a plant, don't pick it*, because if you don't know what it is, you can't possibly know whether it should be picked or protected!

Don't Pick

Any alpine plants	Most woodland plants
Any wild orchids	Barren Strawberry
Any lady slippers	Bloodroot
Most bog plants	Canada Lily
Canada Violet	Pitcher Plant
Cardinal Flower	Purple Gerardia
Downy Yellow Violet	Rattlesnake Plantain
Dutchman's Breeches	Sundew
Fringed Gentian	Swamp Rose Mallow
Hepatica	Trailing Arbutus
Indian Pipe	Trillium
Jack-in-the-pulpit	Turk's-cap Lily
Partridgeberry	Twinflower
Pipsissewa	Wood lily

Do Pick

Asters	Joe-Pye Weed
Black-eyed Susan	Knotweed
Bluets	Meadowsweet
Bouncing Bet	Milkweeds

Butter-and-eggs
Buttercups
Campion
Cattail
Chicory
Cinquefoil
Clover
Coneflower
Daisies
Daisy-fleabane
Evening Primrose
Everlastings
Fireweed
Forget-me-not
Golden Aster
Goldenrods
Hawkweeds
Ironweed
Jewelweed

Pickerelweed
Purple Loosestrife
Queen Anne's Lace
Sheep Laurel
Spreading Dogbane
St. John's-wort
Steeple Bush
Sunflower
Tansy
Thistles
Trefoils
Violets (except those
        in DON'T PICK
        list)
Wild Geranium
Wild Lily-of-the-Valley
Wild Roses
Yarrow
Yellow Loosestrife

Once again, please remember that flowers that do not appear on either of these lists should be left alone, unless you *know* that in your area they may be picked.

CHAPTER 11

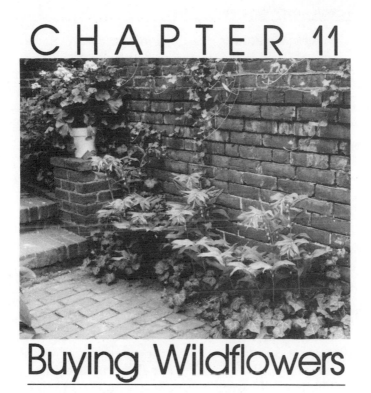

Buying Wildflowers

I made enough mistakes with my first two wildflower purchases to fill a book, and this chapter, at least, is written in the hope that it will keep you from doing the same.

My first mistake was to answer an advertisement in a newspaper for a "Lady Slipper Collection," one each of four varieties, including the almost-impossible-to-grow pink moccasin flower. Actually, all lady slippers are among the most difficult plants for beginners—don't let the description "hardy orchids" mislead you. Hardy refers only to temperature, not temperament. Naturally, the advertisement didn't make any mention of these facts. All it said was that these "hardy orchids" require shade, acid soil, and some moisture, all of which we were prepared to provide. So I ordered my lady slippers, put them in the ground, and never saw them again.

A sort of suberror to that first mistake was to buy one each of a variety of plants. Wildflowers in general like a little company of their own kind, and anyway one plant, unless it is very big or very prolific, doesn't make much of a display.

ABOVE: Solomon's seal in a city garden. *(George Taloumis)*

I wonder why wildflower dealers don't recognize the long-term effect of their emphasis on the glamorous flowers, both in their catalogs and their advertisements. For the price of four expensive lady slippers, I could have bought a dozen plants that would have survived even my ignorance of wildflower gardening. Instead, in what I have since discovered is a typical reaction, I simply concluded that wildflowers were indeed too difficult for an ordinary gardener like myself.

It was some years before I tried my luck again; this time I at least had the sense to write for a catalog. Although hampered by the absence of those brighter-than-life pictures one expects to find in a nursery catalog, as well as my unfamiliarity with most of the flowers listed, I nevertheless put together what sounded like a perfectly delightful wildflower garden—trillium, foamflower, trailing arbutus, bunch-berry, butterfly weed, and cardinal flower. I could hardly wait for the package to arrive.

Determined to do everything right, I prepared myself by borrowing all the books I could find in the library, and when my order arrived, set out with books and plants to create my little woodland garden.

Hours later, I was sadder and wiser: my flowers simply did not go together, and most of them didn't go at all in the bed I had planned for them. The butterfly weed needed a dry sunny site; the cardinal flower, sun but lots of moisture; the trailing arbutus wanted a sandy woods soil and the bunchberry a cool rich woods, and both of them needed more acid soil than I then had. Only the trillium and the foamflower were likely to do well in the spot I had selected for my garden. By the time I had planted each flower in the spot most likely to suit it, I didn't have a wildflower garden at all, but just a half dozen new plants scattered all over the lot.

With this negative introduction to the subject of buying wildflowers, I should hurry up and say that ever since I learned what I was doing, I have had excellent success with purchased plants, at least as good and usually better than with even the most carefully collected spec-imens found in my own locality.

Some wildflower gardeners buy all of their new plants. For others, collecting is half the fun. Even if you are in the latter group, sooner or later you are sure to want to add a plant that you can only get by purchase, because it is protected, or too difficult to transplant from the wild, or because it doesn't grow wild in your part of the country.

Although you will occasionally find potted wildflowers in regular nurseries, or seeds and plants listed in the larger catalogs, for any kind of extensive collection you will really have to deal with specialists.

There are relatively few of these and most of them are located in places you can hardly find on the map, so unless you happen to know a grower in your area, you will be doing most of your buying by mail. Since that is how wildflower dealers do most of their business anyway, they are all geared for this kind of purchasing.

SELECTING A DEALER

It seems only reasonable to assume that the dealer who is nearest you is the best choice, both because his stock of plants is more likely to be native to your area and because the elapsed time between packing and planting will be the shortest. The second consideration has a good deal of validity, although it is not as crucial as you might think. Airmail postage or "special handling" will usually speed the package to you, and every wildflower grower I have bought from is so adept at packaging that my plants have always arrived in excellent condition.

As for buying locally because the plants will be native, this is of minimal importance (provided, of course, that you order plants you can accommodate). As we have repeatedly seen, the same wildflowers grow in any area where climate and soil conditions are similar; some of them are native to many different areas, and some have been established there. In fact, wildflower dealers buy from each other, usually for the same reasons you buy from them—to get plants that don't grow wild in their part of the country. If you read through very many wildflower catalogs, you quickly realize that most of the popular wildflowers are carried by every dealer, whether located in the Northeast, the Northwest, the southern mountain states, or the Middle West.

For a different reason, however, geography should play a part in your selection of a dealer. If you live in a cold northern state where spring doesn't come until late April, and you order plants from a southern grower who starts shipping in February, you'll either get your plants too early or, if you have asked him not to ship until early May, you will receive plants that have already put forth too much tender new growth to be moved with impunity.

So, if all other things are equal, you would do best to buy from the nearest dealer, and second-best from a dealer whose growing seasons correspond with your own.

But all other things are not equal, which is why you should send away for as many catalogs as you can, and if possible order from several dealers before you settle upon a favorite. The reason for this is quite simply that prices vary considerably and from my experience are no indication of quality. I bought ferns last year from two nurseries, one nearby and one a thousand miles away. The ferns from the distant nursery arrived in excellent condition, were considerably larger and stronger than the others, and cost exactly half as much.

Just as price is not an indicator of quality, neither is the glossiness of the catalog an indicator of price. Both of the dealers from whom I bought the ferns publish relatively elaborate catalogs, for wildflower dealers, many of whom will send you what appears to be nothing more than a mimeographed sheet of paper. The best way to judge a wildflower nursery, if you have no personal recommendation, is by what the catalog says, not by what it looks like (although it *is* nice to see pictures of unfamiliar plants).

As a general rule, I think you should avoid dealers who do not list flowers by their Latin as well as their popular names, because you may not get the plant you think you are ordering. I would also avoid the dealer who never warns you that a wildflower is either difficult or has certain specific environmental requirements; in his brochure you are likely to find the phrase "easy to grow in average garden soil" more often than is actually the case. His plants may (or may not) be just as good as the next man's, but I prefer to give my business to those growers who take the trouble to give me as much information as they can about the cultural needs of their plants. Some of the small catalogs are real treasure houses of information on growing wildflowers.

WHEN SHOULD YOU ORDER?

The catalog of a Vermont nursery states, "We cannot overemphasize the importance of shipping wildflowers at the proper season. Autumn is the best time to move practically all wildflowers. They are nearly dormant and will handle best at that time." This grower, who will not fill orders after mid-April, except at the purchaser's risk, points out that wildflowers are usually growing under the frozen surface of the earth long before they can be dug for shipping. By late spring, the young growth is tender and highly perishable. In many cases, however, it will regrow, if it is not too far advanced, or if it is a bulb.

Although virtually every grower stresses the advantage of planting in the fall—some won't even ship trillium and certain other early flowers in the spring—this, like a great many other rules, can be broken. Part of the fun of gardening is spending a few dreary January or February days with the catalogs, and having done that, I haven't the strength of character to wait until the following fall to order plants. It is true that not all of the flowers I plant in the spring bloom the first year, but many of them do, although a little late, to be sure.

In any event, if you order for spring planting, get your order in as early as you possibly can and specify the date when you want your shipment to arrive. It doesn't help to have the plants on hand before your earth is workable. This is a good reason for buying plants from a dealer whose seasons coincide with your own.

Depending on the locale of the nursery, the spring shipping season usually begins in early March and lasts until the middle of May, and northern growers have an even shorter spring season, often no more than a month. So you can see the importance of placing your spring orders early if you want to get them filled. The fall shipping and planting season begins as early as August and lasts until November 1, again depending on the location of the nursery. California and southern growers may ship all year, but of course only to people who can plant all year.

If you don't get around to putting your order in early, allow at least a minimum of three weeks for it to arrive: a week for the mail, back and forth, and two weeks for filling the order. Many of the wildflower nurseries you will be dealing with are small personal or family businesses, and some of them dig the plants, or collect them, as each individual order arrives.

Which brings us to a question I suspect has been on your minds, since I assume that anyone interested in wildflower gardening is equally interested in wildflower conservation—or should be.

It is fairly standard practice for wildflower authors to admonish readers not to buy plants from dealers who collect, only from those who propagate their own plants. Ironically, the same writers who give that advice also publish lists of wildflower dealers—every one of whom collects at least some of the plants he sells. The real issue is how he collects, and where, and what. And the problem is that you really have no way of knowing.

To take the example of the lady slippers once again; if those I bought and killed were nursery-propagated, then it is hard to make the case that any real damage was done to the native lady slipper population. If, on the other hand, they were collected stock, to be sent out to virtually certain death purely for the financial benefit of the seller, then that surely is a crime against conservation. Perhaps the best thing you can do is refuse to order the rare, difficult plants, or ask that another plant be substituted for the lady slipper unless it was nursery-

propagated. (Most of the mail-order nurseries that specialize in inexpensive seedling plants of all kinds also sell a few wild flowers.
These are almost always collected stock, and cannot compare in other
ways either with the plants you get from reputable wildflower specialists.)

Leaving aside the lady slippers and other endangered species, can
one justify any collecting of plants from the wild for purely personal
profit?

In the course of preparing this chapter, I wrote to about twenty-
five wildflower dealers, asking them whether they collected or grew
their own plants, and if they collected, how they justified this activity
in terms of conservation. Admittedly, my question was in the when-
did-you-stop-beating-your-wife category, and their answers would
necessarily be self-serving. Nevertheless, what they said was of considerable interest.

Virtually every dealer who replied said that most of his plants were
propagated on his own land or other private land, or bought from
other dealers. One dealer replied that it is simpler to dig and pack
twelve plants from the garden than to hunt one in the wild.

An Illinois grower said, "The only ones we collect are those in our
area which we have protected from livestock destruction and worked
with and used conservatively over the years. Rather than dig out
completely, we can boast more plants than when we first took over
the project."

As one who thinks of wildflower destruction in terms of roadbuild-
ers and bulldozers, I was surprised at the number of references to
lifestock. "We consider collecting a rescue mission," another dealer
wrote. "Cattle and sheep roam through our forests and loggers destroy
whole areas. Clear-cut logging involves bulldozing. We have no 'protected' lists out here, and if we did, the cattle, sheep, and loggers
can't read!"

Actually, hobby collectors can learn a lot from the growers who
collect plants for sale, and who have an interest in increasing rather
than depleting their stock. Mrs. Clair Phillips of Orchid Gardens in
Minnesota, one of the states that licenses wildflower nurseries, wrote,
"We propagate many species in their native locations to save our time
and space here around the home place, and also to keep the species
pure. We never leave small-sized plants lay to dry out, but reset all
the seedlings and divisions and also plant seed, covering it there as
we find it. We never collect all of a colony of plants, but always leave

plenty of parent stock. The only time we try to deplete an area is when it is to be bulldozed."

MAKING UP YOUR ORDER

Before you get carried away by the catalogs, here are a few general rules:

Be sure you have the right place for the plants you choose; no water-loving plants if you have no water.

If you are ordering a selection of plants for one place in your garden, check to make sure they are compatible with each other, as well as the garden; some woodland plants, for example, need a lot more moisture, acid, or shade than others. Avoid all unnamed collections, including "wildflowers for sun" or "wildflowers for shade." These are rarely worth the bother. Double this warning in spades for seed collections.

Be wary of all "special collections" unless you are familiar with all of the plants in the collection. If even one or two fail, or aren't flowers you like, you haven't bought a bargain. Some day you may want a whole trillium collection, but meanwhile if that group includes the painted trillium, you have a real prima donna on your hands. A "beginner's collection" in front of me includes one each of twenty different plants, including two that are notoriously hard to grow.

Don't buy one each of any plant anyway. Make it a rule to buy at least three of a kind.

If you have failed with a particular wildflower in the past, don't feel that you must try, try again. Maybe there was a good reason why that plant didn't grow. Even if there wasn't, why court discouragement when there are so many others to choose from? Later on, by all means try again if you want to, maybe in a slightly different place, but for now remember that you are doing this for fun, not to prove anything to anyone.

If your budget is tight and your grounds expansive, consider the fast-growing, even invasive plants that you yourself can divide to increase your stock. Just be careful not to choose the ones that can't be eradicated once they take hold, like Japanese honeysuckle. Also consider the plants that reseed freely. And read the section below on buying seeds instead of plants in the first place.

Make a carbon of your order or write it out on a separate sheet of paper, and save it! At the time you send off your check, you may think you'll not forget what you have bought, but by the time the plants arrive, labeled only with their Latin names, you may have a good deal of trouble associating *Medeola virginiana* with Indian cucumber root or *Tiarella cordifolia* with foamflower. Needless to say, you should write both the Latin and the English names of your plants on your list. I also find it helpful, if I have ordered plants for more than one area, to make a note next to the flower indicating what bed it is destined for.

WILL DEALERS FILL ORDERS FOR UNSUITABLE PLANTS?

I asked the growers whether, if you ordered a plant unlikely to survive in your area, they would fill the order. The answer is, yes, they will. After all, they have no way of knowing whether you have ordered out of ignorance or out of such expertise that you may have found some special way of ensuring the survival of the plants. Mrs. Phillips points out that while extreme southern states like Texas and Florida are not suited to their cold-climate plants, a few people in those areas have devised ways of giving artificial cold during a dormant period. Some people use them in terrariums. Most of the larger growers ship to every state in the Union, including Alaska and Hawaii.

On the other hand, when you ask the grower to make a substitution if you seem to have ordered an unsuitable plant, most of them will be glad to do so. Wildflower growers are very generous about giving advice, but do write, if you must, in the off-seasons and be sure to enclose a stamped, addressed return envelope.

WHEN YOUR PLANTS ARRIVE

If your wildflowers are to be planted in a special bed—a woodland garden, a rock garden, an artificial pool or bog, or the like—your bed must be prepared before the plants arrive. If you have ordered plants for a regular garden bed or for your foundation planting, there may not be any extensive preparation. Still, wherever you plan to put the wildflowers, be sure that they can be planted right away. Unlike potted plants that can wait a few days or even more if necessary, these have already been out of the ground and traveling for some time. Actually, I find I am constantly surprised at how beautifully the plants do survive shipment. I also get an extra bit of pleasure out of the box that comes from the wildflower grower, which has nothing to do with the contents. In a day when everything comes wrapped with such packaging overkill—the unopenable, indisposable package protecting an unbreakable object—it is a joy to get a plain, sturdy cardboard box tied with what I am sure used to be called stout cord. You can untie the cord and even re-use it, and you can open the box without a knife, a screwdriver, and a box of Band-aids.

Within the package, your plants should be wrapped by species and labeled. Most growers use sphagnum moss and black plastic. If your plants are not in good condition when they arrive, or if the package has been damaged in transit, save everything and notify the nursery immediately. Growers do not guarantee the fate of their plants once they have been delivered in good condition—obviously they have no control over what you or nature does with them—but they do guarantee that you will receive healthy, well-packaged plants.

If you cannot plant your wildflowers as soon as you get them, because of bad weather, a head cold, or company coming for dinner, open the box immediately and put it in a cool shaded place. Keep the roots covered with soil or moss, and don't let them dry out. Don't let them get soggy either, particularly if they are wrapped in plastic.

BUYING WILDFLOWER SEEDS

A number of my friends, knowing of my interest in wildflower gardening, have asked me where they could buy packages of seeds "to scatter about" their country properties. Although I admire their intent, I always discourage them from scattering seeds about; only the most minute fraction of the seeds that are propagated that way in nature ever manage to survive. If you want to grow flowers from seed, you should be prepared to give them as much of a chance for survival as you would the seeds of any cultivated flower, following the directions on the package.

If you do buy seeds, by all means avoid "mixed" packages, usually called "wildflowers for sun" or "wildflowers for shade." The flowers aren't likely to be very good to start with, and probably don't have the same germination requirements; if anything grows, it's sure to be the weedy or very strong varieties only. The other thing to be wary of—a new phenomenon so far as I know, and one that is probably going to turn out to be very popular as wildflower growing increases in popularity—are the beautiful gift packages of named wildflower seeds. I first saw these in a large New England nursery last winter just before Christmas, and I was enchanted with the thought of giving them as gifts myself. When I looked at the different packages, however, I realized that there wasn't one flower that could be expected to grow in the humid East. Sure enough, the address of the company was in one of the dry western Plains states. It's a lovely idea, but be careful.

In the past few years, more and more "regular" seed catalogs are including some wildflower seeds. Most of these, of course, are wildflowers that have become staples of the cultivated garden, like *Phlox divaricata* or Virginia bluebell. Once in a while, the names have been tidied up for inclusion in these garden catalogs—as in the case of butterfly weed, which has become butterfly flower in one catalog. Once again, this is an argument for including the plant's Latin name in your order. If it's *Asclepias tuberosa*, you know it's butterfly weed, no matter what else it is called.

WILDFLOWER DEALERS

The list below is by no means inclusive. I have tried to restrict myself to nurseries that propagate their own plants rather than collecting them, and to those that fill mail orders. But there surely are many nurseries that do both, which I do not know. For an up-to-date comprehensive list of sources for wildflowers and other native plants, I suggest you send $3.50 to the New England Wild Flower Society, Garden in the Woods, Hemenway Road, Framingham, MA 01701. Their list of almost 200 sources is broken down by region of the country.

Albright & Towne, Inc.
5143 Port Chicago Highway
Concord, CA 94520
(seeds)

Allgrove
Box 4590
Wilmington, MA 01887
(plants)

Appalachian Wildflower Nursery
Route 1, Box 275 A
Reedsville, PA 17084
(plants, some seeds)

Arkansas Valley Seed, Inc.
P.O. Box 270
Rocky Ford, CO 81067
(seeds)

Boehlke's Woodland Gardens
W 140 N 10829 Country Aire Road
Germantown, WI 53022
(plants)

Browning's Nursery
Sixes, OR 97476
(plants and seeds)

Conley's Garden Center
Boothbay Harbor, ME 04538
(plants and seeds)

Daystar
Rt 2, Box 250
Litchfield, ME 04350
(plants)

Desert Enterprises
P.O. Box 23
Morristown, AZ 85342
(seeds)

Far North Gardens
16785 Harrison Street
Livonia, MI 48154
(seeds, some plants)

Gardens of the Blue Ridge
US 221 N
Pineola, NC 28662
(plants, including some collected)

WILDFLOWER DEALERS (continued)

Great Lakes Wildflowers
Box 1923
Milwaukee, WI 53201
(plants)

Horticultural Systems Inc.
P.O. Box 70
Parrish, FL 33564
(seeds, some plants)

Hubbs Brothers Seed Company
1015 N. 35th Street
Phoenix, AZ 85008
(seeds)

J.L. Hudson Seedsman
P.O. Box 1058
Redwood City, CA 94064
(seeds)

LaFayette Home Nursery, Inc.
RR 1, Box 1A
LaFayette, IL 61449
(prairie seeds)

Las Pilitas Nursery
Star Route, Box 23X
Santa Margarita, CA 93453
(plants and seeds)

Lofts, Inc.
Chimney Rock Road
Bound Brook, NJ 08805
(seeds)

Midwest Wildflowers
Box 64
Rockton, IL 61072
(seeds)

Native Plant Nursery, Inc.
9180 S. Wasatch Blvd.
Sandy, UT 84092
(plants)

Natural Habitat Nursery
4818 Terminal Road
McFarland, WI 53558
(seeds)

New Mexico Native Plants Nursery
309 West College
Silver City, NM 88061
(seeds)

L.L. Olds Seed Company
Box 7790
Madison, WI 53707
(seeds)

Orchid Gardens
6700 Splithand Road
Grand Rapids, MN 55744
(plants, including some collected)

Passiflora
Rt 1, Box 190A
Germantown, NC 27019
(seeds)

Plants of the Southwest
1570 Pacheco Street
Santa Fe, NM 87501
(plants and seeds)

Prairie Moon Nursery
Box 163, Route 3
Winona, MN 55987
(seeds)

WILDFLOWER DEALERS (continued)

Prairie Nursery
Box 365, Route 1
Westfield, WI 53564
(plants and seeds)

Prairie Ridge Nursery
9738 Overland Road
Mount Horeb, WI 53572
(plants and seeds)

Prairie Seed Source
P.O. Box 83
North Lake, WI 53064
(seeds)

Putney Nursery, Inc.
Putney, VT 05346
(plants, including some collected)

Redwood Nursery
2800 El Rancho Drive
Santa Cruz, CA 95060
(plants and seeds)

S & R Seed Company, Inc.
Box 86
Cass Lake, MN 56633
(seeds)

Sharp Brothers Seed Co.
P.O. Box 140
Healy, KS 67850
(seeds)

Southwestern Native Seeds
Box 50503
Tucson, AZ 85703
(seeds)

Dean E. Swift
P.O. Box B
Jaroso, CO 81138
(seeds)

Twin Peaks Seeds
12721 Avenue de Espuela
Poway, CA 92064
(seeds)

Wildwood Farm
10300 Sonoma Highway
Kenwood, CA 95452
(plants)

Yerba-Buena Nursery
19500 Skyline Blvd.
Woodside, CA 94062
(plants)

SELECTED BIBLIOGRAPHY

Berglund, Berndt, and Bolsby, Clare E. *The Edible Wild*. N. Y.: Charles
  Scribner's Sons, 1971.
Cobb, Boughton. *A Field Guide to the Ferns and their Related Families
  (Northeastern and Central North America)*, Peterson Field Guide Se-
  ries. Boston: Houghton Mifflin Co., 1956.
Dietz, Marjorie J. *The Concise Encyclopedia of Favorite Wild Flowers*.
  Garden City: Doubleday & Co., 1965.
Flemer, William III. *Nature's Guide to Successful Gardening and Land-
  scaping*. N.Y.: Thomas Y. Crowell Co., 1972.
Foley, Daniel J. *Gardening By the Sea*. Philadelphia: Chilton Co., 1965.
Foster, F. Gordon. *Ferns to Know and Grow*. N.Y.: Hawthorn Books,
  1971.
Gardening in the Shade. Handbook of the Brooklyn Botanic Garden,
  1971.

Gardening with Native Plants. Handbook of the Brooklyn Botanic Garden, 1962.

Gibbons, Euell. *Stalking the Wild Asparagus.* N.Y.: David McKay Co., 1962.

Gleason, Henry A., and Cronquist, Arthur. *The Natural Geography of Plants.* N.Y.: Columbia University Press, 1964.

Handbook on Ferns. Brooklyn Botanic Gardens, 1969.

Hersey, Jean. *Wild Flowers to Know and Grow.* Princeton: D. Van Nostrand Co., 1964.

Hinds, Harold R., and Hathaway, Wildred A. *Wildflowers of Cape Cod.* Chatham, Mass.: Chatham Press, 1968.

House, Homer D. *Wild Flowers of New York* (2 vols.). Albany: University of the State of New York, 1919.

Hull, Helen S. *Wild Flowers for Your Garden.* N. Y.: Gramercy Publishing Co., 1932.

Kingsbury, John M. *Poisonous Plants of the United States and Canada.* Englewood Cliffs, N.J.: Prentice-Hall, 1964.

Peterson, Roger Tory, and McKenny, Margaret. *A Field Guide to Wildflowers of Northeastern and North-central North America* (Peterson Field Guide Series). Boston: Houghton Mifflin Co., 1968.

Petry, Loren C. *A Beachcomber's Botany.* Chatham, Mass.: The Chatham Conservation Foundation, 1968.

Reid, G. *How to Hold Up a Bank.* Cranbury, N. J.: A. S. Barnes, 1970.

Sterling, Dorothy. *The Outer Lands.* N.Y.: Natural History Press, 1967.

Taylor, Kathryn S., and Hamblin, Stephen F. *Handbook of Wild Flower Cultivation.* N.Y.: Macmillan Co., 1963.

The Salty Thumb. Montauk Village Association, Montauk, L.I., N.Y., 1967.

Wyman, Donald. *Ground Cover Plants.* N.Y.: Macmillan Co., 1956.

INDEX